Contents

Acknowledgments

DEDICATION

I dedicate this book to my
husband, Jack McDonald III,
and to my children, Ashby
and Jack IV. Thanks for
believing in me, loving me,
and persevering with me.

*"Some trust in chariots and some
in horses, but we trust in the name
of the Lord our God."*

Psalm 20:7

I would like to thank the following people: Mr. and Mrs. M.
Pierce Ashby, for purchasing my first pony, Duke, and enabling
me to earn a bachelor's degree in animal science from Virginia
Polytechnic Institute and State University; Mrs. Catherine Ashby
Akins, for her invaluable contributions and support; Mr. Charlie
D. Akins, for taking me to my first horse show; Mrs. Pat Betts, for
giving me my first riding lessons and teaching me and hundreds of
others how to ride properly; Mrs. Susan DeVries, English
professor, Day Star University, Nairobi, Kenya; Mr. Joe Fargis,
for teaching me how to "equitate" as a "junior," and, along with
Conrad Homfeld, being my first employer in the horse business;
Ms. Kathy Farrow; Sarah Fletcher, M.D.; and Dr. A.N. Huff.
"Building a User Base" is adapted from the article, "Horse
Marketing: Expanding the User Base," May 1988, written by
Dr. A.N. Huff, Extension animal scientist emeritus, and is used
with his permission. Sections on breeding are adapted from *The
Selection and Promotion of the Breeding Stallion*, by Steve G. Jennings.
This excellent self-published book is available through S.J.
Publications, P.O. Box 615, Front Royal, VA 22630; I would also
like to thank Betty, Mike, and Tim Jennings, of Professional
Auction Services, Inc.; Ms. Maribel Koella, a partner with Collins,
Sharp & Koella; Melissa Aberle Johnson; Pam Marks, Marks
Insurance and Associates, Inc., Germantown, Maryland;
Dr. Thomas N. Meacham; Mr. Jack McDonald III, Chartered
Financial Analyst; Ms. Trish Palys, equestrian trainer;
Ms. Barbara Person, equine insurance specialist; Mrs. Susan
Smith; Daniel W. Sutherland and Mrs. Elise J. Sutherland;
Ms. Susan Terranella, manager, Rio Vista Farm, Leander, Texas;
Mrs. Carla McDonald Thomas, President, Board of Directors,
Tennessee Valley Hunt; Dea Kelly Thomas, Master of Foxhounds,
Tennessee Valley Hunt; Mrs. Alexander W. Wallace, owner of
Medway Ranch, for having faith in me and giving me the opportu-
nity to manage her ranch; and Dr. Nathaniel White, Marion
Dupont Equine Medical Center, Leesburg, Virginia.

Starting & Running Your Own

HORSE BUSINESS

Mary Ashby McDonald

STOREY
BOOKS

*The mission of Storey Publishing is to serve our customers
by publishing practical information that encourages
personal independence in harmony with the environment.*

Edited by Diana Delmar and Elizabeth McHale
Design, production, and editorial assistance by Meredith Maker
Production assistance by Erin Lincourt and Allyson L. Hayes
Cover photograph © Grant Heilman Photography, by Alix Coleman
Line drawings by Brigita Fuhrmann; illustration on page 30 is adapted from an original by Pam Talley Stoneburner
Indexed by Susan Olason, Indexes & Knowledge Maps

The information in this book is true and complete to the best of our knowledge. All recommendations are made without guarantee on the part of the author or Storey Publishing. The author and publisher disclaim any liability in connection with the use of this information. For additional information, please contact Storey Books, 210 MASS MoCA Way, North Adams, MA 01247.

Storey Books are available for special premium and promotional uses and for customized editions. For further information, please call Storey's Custom Publishing Department at 1-800-793-9396.

Printed in Canada by Interglobe
10 9 8

Library of Congress Cataloging-in-Publication Data

McDonald, Mary Ashby, 1959–
    Starting and running your own horse business / by Mary Ashby McDonald.
        p.   cm.

    Includes index.
    ISBN 0-88266-960-5 (pb : alk. paper)
    1. Horse farms—Management.   2. Stables—Management.
    3. New business enterprises.   4. Small business—Management. I. Title.
SF291.M384   1997
636.1'0068—dc21   96-49470
                                                CIP

Introduction

This book is designed for anyone interested in reducing expenses and making money in the horse business. Some people will say this is an unrealistic notion, but it really *is* possible to keep costs down and maintain a positive cash flow.

In 1982, I took over management of the Medway Ranch in Austin, Texas. The ranch was practically unknown to the public. There was no letterhead, logo, colors, brochures — not even an ad in the Yellow Pages. Through the application of sound business practices, including an advertising and promotion campaign, the ranch turned into a respected, profitable enterprise in just a few years.

By making a horse business successful, we reap more than just monetary reward. We can better appreciate the many pleasures that attracted us in the first place. There is the gratification of walking into a clean barn, where well-kept horses are munching on sweet-smelling hay. Do you remember the first time one of your green horses accomplished a flying lead change? Or the delight in the eyes of a parent whose young son received his certificate for horsemanship at summer day camp? How about the students who come to you as beginners and ultimately win a handful of ribbons at a show, or the tremendous pride you feel when one of your horses or students progresses to the U.S. Equestrian Team! These are the joys that make laboring through the hot days of summer and frigid winter nights in the barn worth the effort — and make you grateful you don't have a desk job. Some of us believe it's the ultimate in mixing business with pleasure.

Whether you own or board one horse or 100, the goals of this book are to provide you with many ways to save money, labor, and time, and to make your job easier and more profitable. As you read, keep a list of the ideas that you would like to use in your own operation. Put an expected date of completion next to each entry on your list, then follow through.

Here's wishing you the best with your business.

> ♘ *By making a horse business successful, we reap more than just monetary reward. We can better appreciate the many pleasures that attracted us in the first place.*

1
Creating an Image

To make your business a success, it must have an image. The image you develop for your enterprise should appeal to current clients and help attract future ones. There are tools and equipment to help you develop an image and get the word out about your business.

NAME YOUR FARM

If you haven't already done so, give your farm a name. Try to select one that people can easily pronounce and remember. Avoid names that could be mistaken for another type of business, such as *McDonald's*. Your farm's name should indicate not only that your business is about horses, but what kind of horse business you operate. Center Line Stables, for instance, would indicate a dressage stable, while Rodeo Ridge Ranch would make it clear the barn is Western. If riding lessons will be the major focus of your business, you may want a name with "school" in the title. For horse businesses that offer all types of riding, a more general name, such as Springfield Riding Center, would be more appropriate.

CHOOSE FARM COLORS

When selecting farm colors, pick tasteful colors that are widely available. I once made the mistake of choosing terra cotta and beige for a farm in Texas that I managed. Have you ever tried to find a blanket or halter in terra cotta and beige? It didn't take long for me to realize that I needed a different color scheme, so I changed to red and white.

Whenever you can, select barn equipment, such as buckets and hay nets, in the colors of your farm or use colored tape to identify your equipment; this helps you keep track of it at horse shows and other events.

DESIGN A LOGO

A logo is another way to develop an image and promote your business. Unless you happen to be a graphic artist, have a professional designer create your business logo. Explain that you want an eye-catching, memorable logo that defines your business. Ask for one with clarity in design so that it can be reduced in size for use on business cards or enlarged for roadside signs or banners.

Design an eye-catching logo, such as this one, and use it widely to promote your business on brochures, newsletters, posters, and so on.

Obtain ownership of the logo so that you can use it freely throughout the life of the farm. If the artist retains ownership, you could be charged a fee each time the logo is used. The initial cost of having a logo designed may seem high, but it's well worth the price once you see how widely it can be used to promote your business.

PUT YOUR IMAGE TO WORK

Once you have a name for your barn, colors, and a logo, what do you do next? Use them on everything, including brochures, newsletters, letterhead, envelopes, invoices, prize lists, posters, and even coolers and blankets. Following are some business tools on which your barn's name, logo, and colors should be prominent.

Use Business Cards

These are essential. Carry them with you always and distribute them freely. Network. Include all pertinent information on the cards, but at the same time not so much information that they look crowded and unprofessional.

Brochures

Your farm should have an attractive brochure that tells readers what it has to offer. Hand the brochures out to prospective clients and keep some in the office where they will be available to visitors.

Business cards should include all pertinent information such as the card on the left — but should not look too crowded, like the card on the right.

Have a professional assist with the wording, layout, and graphics. Before you begin to design it, think about the quality of your product. Do you need a flashy brochure with color photographs, or would it suffice to have a simple but attractive black-and-white brochure with just enough type to sell your goods and services? The brochure should include the following information:

- Name of your business
- Brief description of your operation
- List of services available
- Names of the owner, manager, and instructors
- Location and map
- Address, phone number, fax number, and e-mail address
- Pictures — the most effective part of any brochure
- Logo, and farm colors if it is a color brochure

Post Signs

Once you purchase these business tools and start putting them to use, you'll want to display your barn's name and logo where it can be seen by a larger audience. Signs along the road work well because they get the name of your business before the community and can be used to direct potential clients to your farm. Here are some pointers to consider when creating and posting signs:

Post signs on your property. If you need to use adjacent land belonging to another party, always obtain written permission. Check with your local zoning board for regulations governing the placement of road signs.

Place signs in plain view near a well-trafficked street, at the intersection of a major roadway, if possible. Smaller signs with indicator arrows may also help steer visitors toward the farm.

Make the message on the sign brief, informative, and large enough to be read from a distance. Ideally, it should include the business name, owner, and a phone number. You may want to include some services you provide ("trail rides," for example).

Construct the sign from long-lasting, weatherproof material and embed the supports in concrete to avoid replacing it every few years.

Consider the shape and size of your sign. The most effective sign for a horse operation includes the image of a horse. One of the most eye-catching and impressive signs I have ever seen was in the shape of a full-sized jumping horse and attached to the property fence. To a driver approaching the farm, the horse appeared to be jumping out of the pasture. As you got closer, you could read the name of the farm, the address, and phone number on the horse.

This eye-catching sign of a horse-shaped figure appears to be jumping out of the pasture.

Place a sign on the sides of your vehicles. Put the name of your farm, your telephone number, and logo on the sides of your cars, trucks, and trailers; either paint it on or use a removable, magnetic sign. This way, you are promoting your business wherever you drive, and your vehicles frequent areas you want to target: feed stores, veterinary offices, tack shops, and horse shows. While painting the information on vehicles looks more professional and lasts longer, magnetic signs are useful if you don't want your logo permanently affixed to your family car: Teenagers and mothers-in-law aren't always excited about driving around in a car that's advertising horses.

INVEST IN GOOD TELEPHONE AND ANSWERING EQUIPMENT

How many times have you called a horse barn and no one answered the phone? Or the person who answered was unfamiliar with the barn's operation, or didn't take the message correctly? Perhaps when the phone was answered the horses were neighing, the tractor was running, or the farrier was pounding, and you hung up feeling frustrated. Frustrated callers are left with a poor impression of the barn and may take their business elsewhere.

There are few pieces of office equipment that are as crucial to your business as an adequate telephone system. If you select wisely, you'll be accessible to current or potential clients, be able to conduct business when necessary, and convey the image of a well-run operation.

Install at least one telephone in your barn as well as in your office. Select quality equipment that will last. Built-in speaker phones allow you to have conference calls with the veterinarian and the client. Portable telephones allow you to have mobility and cellular telephones and beepers enable

Hang a bulletin board and blackboard for activities or messages near the telephone in the barn.

Today's Classes:

DON'T FORGET YOUR HELMETS!

someone to reach you in an emergency during foaling season. These can be expensive, so figure out first if they are necessary and worth the investment.

Telephone Tips

The following suggestions will help you to be more accessible to current or potential clients:

- Have pen and paper secured next to each telephone. Keep your calendar and a list of upcoming events, teaching dates, and horses for sale near the phone to avoid missing any business opportunities.
- Instruct people who answer the telephone to do so professionally. They should state the name of the farm, give their name, and ask how they can help the caller.
- If students, boarders, and visitors to the farm often tie up your business line and run up the telephone bill, consider installing a pay phone for them to use or only make available local service and use a calling card for your long distance calls.
- The answering machine is an important extension of the telephone. Check the recommendations in *Consumer Guide Reports* and buy a machine that will last. It will pay for itself by preventing lost business. An answering machine will allow you to screen calls while conducting other business, and remote control options allow you to listen to or leave messages from another location. They are invaluable for staff communication ("I'll feed the horses in the morning," or "Expect a feed delivery tomorrow"). Machines that record the date and time of messages are particularly useful when students call in to cancel a lesson.
- Record a clear, brief, informative message on your answering machine. Change outdated messages promptly. If you receive many calls inquiring about which services you offer, you may want to mention the services you provide on the tape. For example, "We specialize in English and Western riding lessons and weekly trail rides."

♘ *When no one is there to answer the phone and messages are left on the machine, schedule a time of day to return calls. Returning calls efficiently promotes the image of a well-run business.*

2
Advertising and Promoting Your Business

There are a number of ways to promote your business, and many of them are described below. Adopt only those that will enhance your business in the immediate future. You can initiate other promotional programs later, as you need them.

NEWSLETTERS

Create an annual, quarterly, or monthly newsletter for students, boarders, other farms, feed stores, veterinary offices, and guests to communicate with others and promote your business. Include the successful activities that have taken place at your farm and exciting upcoming events. People enjoy seeing news about themselves and their horses in print. Take a few photographs of students with their favorite equines and have the local print shop screen them into the newsletter. If you plan to buy a computer, software, and printer, consider equipment that will enable you to produce your own newsletters.

You also can include:
- Upcoming riding events — shows, clinics, short courses, and trail rides
- Horses for sale
- Inoculation and worming schedules
- Informative articles, quotes, poems, cartoons, and crossword puzzles
- Special services — clipping, spring blanket washing, trailering services, etc.
- Special awards — rider of the month, employee of the month, emergency dismount of the month, horse or dog of the month
- Tack shop specials
- Barn socials

Ten Oaks Riding Center

Fall 1999

Thanksgiving Weekend Schooling Show Planned

Be sure to sign up for our annual schooling show held the day after Thanksgiving. This is a great learning opportunity for students who aspire to our show team, and for the more experienced among us who want to polish their skills.

The show begins at 8 a.m. There will be concession stands to help raise money for the show team. Invite your family and friends! Details are in the barn office.

Scenic Fall Trail Ride for Adults

A two-hour trail ride for adults is planned for October 5 so we can enjoy the fall landscape. There will be two groups: One is for beginners, who will walk/trot, and the other is for intermediate riders, who will walk/trot/canter.

We'll leave at 10 a.m., and when we return, have a picnic. Everyone is asked to contribute a dish. Sign up in the office!

Plan Your Costumes: It's Halloween Time!

The children's Halloween party will start at 6 p.m. on Oct. 29. We'll play games, including an apple bob, and have refreshments. We'll conclude the evening with a parade of students and their favorite horses, all in costume. Prizes will be awarded for the best student/horse team.

Summer Camp Concludes With Record Numbers

We had over 100 students in our summer camp this year — the highest number ever! Students ranged in age from 8 to 18. Most were beginners when they started their two-week sessions, but by the time they finished, they were all posting to the trot, and some were even cantering with ease. Several have enrolled in our regular riding school.

Winter Tack Shop Sale!

Winter will be here before you know it, so be prepared. The price of all winter riding clothes in the tack shop will be 10% off through the month of October.

Ten Oaks students get 15% off.

Turn the page for show news!!

Trail Riders: Safety First!

Hunting season is here. Bow hunting is permitted throughout most of the fall and beyond Christmas, and deer hunters with guns begin hunting around Thanksgiving weekend.

Trail riders should avoid riding at dusk or dawn. They should wear bright colors. We also advise carrying bells. Orange riding vests and bells are available in our tack shop.

Producing a newsletter will help you publicize events and activities at your horse business.

Promotional Material

Remember, the type of promotional material you produce reflects the *quality* of your business. You want to have the best business cards, brochures, newsletters, and stationery you can afford. Strive for excellence without extravagance; save on costs without sacrificing quality.

- At shows, clinics, or around the holidays, arrange to have a professional photographer take pictures of students and boarders in riding clothes with their horses. Offer the photographer the opportunity to take individual portraits and sell them to the students and boarders. In return, ask the photographer to provide, at no cost or at a discount, scenes from the farm that you could use in your brochure.

- Comparison shop for printing. Some printers use colored ink on certain days for the same price as black and white.
- Buy in bulk and get the most for your money. For instance, the cost of printing 1,000 business cards or brochures may be much less per piece than the cost of having 100 items printed at a time. Estimate if you want the supply of brochures, business cards, or other items to last one year, two years, or more, then order accordingly. Don't include specific prices or schedules of events in promotional materials such as the brochure or they'll soon be outdated.
- Keep printing costs low by typesetting on your own computer.
- Always proofread the copy of printed material before it goes to press, and save your initialed receipt. I once proofed a piece before it went to print and made sure there were no errors. The typesetter then omitted a word. Because I could prove it was the printer's error, I got the material for half price.
- Develop a good relationship with a quality printer and that printer may be willing to donate trophies and/or buy advertisements in horse show programs.

PROMOTIONAL GOODS AND GIFTS

Invest in tastefully designed bumper stickers, T-shirts, sweatshirts, jackets, key chains, baseball caps, sun visors, dog coats, grooming aprons, pens, memo pads, or magnets. Sell the more expensive items to cover your costs, and give away the smaller ones as promotional gifts to prospective students or boarders. Give them to people from other farms who buy a horse from you so they don't forget your farm name. Come up with a new slogan every year. Hold a contest annually in which students and boarders provide suggestions, then award a prize to the one who comes up with the best suggestion.

COMMERCIAL ADVERTISING AND PROMOTION

Passing out business cards, brochures, and newsletters and putting your colors and logo on your signs, equipment, and vehicles will all help promote your business, but commercial advertising and

GET YOUR NAME OUT THERE!

Here are some suggestions for promotional slogans and bumper stickers:

I jump for
Ten Oaks Riding Center.

•

Ten Oaks Riding Center
is a stable place.

•

Let's horse around at
Ten Oaks Riding Center.

•

My other car is a horse at
Ten Oaks Riding Center.

•

Have you hugged your horse at
Ten Oaks Riding Center today?

•

I'd rather be riding at
Ten Oaks Riding Center.

•

Ten Oaks Riding Center
Horse Show Team

•

Ten Oaks Riding Center
Summer Day Camp

•

Ten Oaks Riding Center
Riding Instructor

•

Ten Oaks Riding Center
Staff

Invest in promotional items, such as baseball caps, T-shirts, coffee mugs, and key chains.

promotion also are necessary to ensure success. The five primary sources for advertising are newspapers, specialty magazines, telephone books, television, and radio. Following are some pointers for advertising in each medium.

Newspapers

Major city newspapers have the broadest circulation and, as a result, are an expensive place to advertise. Local newspapers or weekly papers are less expensive and, because they often need your advertising dollars, are usually more willing to negotiate good deals. Advertising in high school and college newspapers, particularly those that have a riding program, are even more inexpensive and may target the specific age group you want to reach; this also promotes goodwill for your business with the students and faculty.

Regardless of the newspaper you choose to advertise in, take the time to establish a rapport with one person on the staff. Ask this person to inform you about upcoming articles that discuss horses favorably, and advertise in that issue, preferably near the article. To reach newcomers in the area, run a small monthly or weekly ad in the classified advertising section; include a short list of

Keep advertisements brief and inviting.

the services you provide, such as lessons and boarding. Always negotiate for the best advertising rates. Here are some examples of how publicity can be good for your business.

- Barbara gets home after schooling her big bay hunter. She picks up the newspaper and sees the write-up in the sports page about the Ten Oaks Riding Center Horse Show. She decides to enter her horse in the next show at the farm.
- Linda has just moved to the area from out of state, but hasn't yet moved her horse, Moses. She sees the results from the show in the newspaper and calls the farm to see if it offers boarding.
- Melissa is in her pajamas, sipping a cup of coffee. She glances through the sports section and notices the results of the horse show. The daughter of her best friend won a ribbon. She decides to sign up her own daughter, Elizabeth, for lessons at the farm.

$

Money-Saving Tip

Get free "advertising" for your farm by sending press releases to your local newspaper. Neatly type up the results of an event or information about an upcoming event, and chances are good that your local newspaper will publish them.

- Charlie has been looking for a more experienced horse for his wife. After seeing the article, he contacts the farm to see what's available.

A press release may not only bring in new business, but it also can build confidence among riders at your barn when they see their names in print.

Invite the press to visit your barn, camp, lessons, clinics, and shows. Perhaps a reporter will want to write a feature article about your farm, complete with photos. This is terrific free advertising. You may get new clients as a result, and press coverage will no doubt be better in the future.

Specialty Magazines

Advertise your horses, products, or events in magazines. Specialty magazines are the most effective since they reach the audience you want to target; you'll get a better return for your money than you would by advertising in publications that go to a lot of people you do not need to reach. For instance, a local children's magazine is a good choice if you are advertising summer day camp or a riding program for children. For advertising horses or horse-related products, run your ad in a horse magazine.

Often, people are impressed when someone selling a horse takes on the expense of advertising in a well-known magazine. I know a horse trader who had been trying to sell a hunter for several months. Some people came out to see the horse, but no one was very interested. The trader then advertised in *The Chronicle of the Horse* magazine, and raised the price of the horse to cover the cost. Someone who had rejected the horse before now saw it advertised in this magazine, came back, and paid the higher price.

Telephone Book

Day in and day out, you probably will receive more calls from people who have seen your name in the telephone book than any other place. List your name in as many sections and in as many ways as you can in the phone book. The white pages are free. Try to list your name, the name of the farm, the camp, and the tack shop.

The Yellow Pages can be costly. Some people searching for barns will look under "Riding Instruction"; others may turn to "Horses." You'll want to list under both, so negotiate getting several listings for one price, or at least at a discount on the listings.

Check out the ads run by competitors to see what you can do to make yours more eye-catching. Print the ad in **bold** or use a decorative border; both will draw attention to your ad without running up the cost substantially.

If the profit from the sale of a horse is sufficient, run an ad in the magazine congratulating the new owner. It helps build goodwill toward your farm. It is also one more opportunity to get the name of your business out with the message that you sell horses.

Television and Radio

The cost of advertising in larger, more well-known television and radio stations is prohibitive for most horse farms. The exception may be public and cable television stations and small, local radio stations, which often welcome the opportunity to announce events in their area, and do so free of charge. Routinely send them announcements about activities at your farm. They might even come out and cover your event.

It is difficult to know exactly how much you should spend on advertising. Don't spend more than you can afford, but be sure to set aside some money for advertising. Build that into your annual budget or, better yet, your business plan. Word of mouth is effective, but advertising reaches thousands of households, many of which may contain horse lovers.

PUBLIC RELATIONS

There are many other ways to promote and build your business besides advertising commercially. One of them is to boost public relations by hosting activities. Here are some ideas:

- Host camp-outs.
- Participate in "career days" offered by many high schools to acquaint students with stable management or certified riding instruction. Students can come to the barn or a riding instructor can speak at the school.
- Donate lessons for a charitable group's raffle or auction. Your donation might be deductible and, ultimately, could bring in more students.
- Hold a seminar on buying a horse. Ask a veterinarian to donate his or her time to explain potential problems to watch out for. Ask an instructor to talk about buying a horse to match the rider's experience level. Advertise the seminar at your local community college and high school and charge a nominal fee for attending.
- Host a party for exhibitors after they participate in a horse show or clinic.
- Hold an open-house and have hands-on demonstrations on clipping, tacking up a horse, and a riding demonstration. For many people, it will be the first time they've ever been near a horse.
- Hold fund-raisers. Organize a theme horse show such as a Christmas show where all participants bring a horse-related gift under $10 to be donated to a local equine rescue league. Or hold a trail ride and donate the profits to charity. In 1985, I helped organize a 20-mile ride to the capital of Texas.

Each rider got pledges for each mile ridden and the profits went to World Vision, a relief organization. We raised over $2,000, which was used to aid earthquake victims in Mexico.

- Participate in international riding exchange programs to expose riders from other countries to your operation. This will give you an opportunity to host a dinner to bring riders together or, if the riders are qualified, a teaching clinic where they can share teaching methods. (See International Riding Programs in Chapter 5.)
- Organize parties to paint jumps or clean school tack. At tack parties, hold contests for students to see who can put together a bridle the fastest or have mock inspections for "cleanest tack." Give away inexpensive prizes such as hoof picks or your farm bumper stickers to the winners. These parties will foster camaraderie as students swap horse tales and have fun. Provide popcorn and drinks or have a "build your own ice cream sundae bar."
- Offer a loss-leader program, such as a session of lessons at below your cost, which may lead to additional profitable business. For example, you can offer a session of lessons to the YMCA at an introductory, reduced rate. After the session is over, some of these students may continue taking lessons at the regular cost.
- Host mock fox hunts. (See Chapter 7 for details.)
- Host square dances or scavenger hunts.
- Host a video night. Select either educational or entertaining horse-related videos.

BUILDING A USER BASE

If the horse business is going to survive and be profitable in the future, those in the business need not only satisfy their current market of clients, but also expand their clientele to get more people involved with horses. This will require both individual and collective efforts among those in the horse business.

People enjoy horses for many reasons, including business, sport, and recreation. Recreation accounts for about 80 percent of horse ownership. Around 40 percent of these horses and ponies are owned or ridden by youth. This leads to some obvious conclusions about marketing and the potential for expanding our user base.

You and others in the horse industry can convey to the public, through advertising, promotion, and public relations activities, the message that horses are enjoyable to people of all ages. Horseback riding is a sport you can begin as an adult and continue to improve. Following are a few ways to expand the industry's user base. Once you have reviewed the ideas, get together with others in the industry to talk about them, and discuss how to implement them in your locality and state.

- Do cross-promotion with public riding stables where rentals are available with basic instruction.
- Help to maintain and support riding areas, trails, and public horse-use facilities, especially in urban and suburban areas.
- Develop and implement urban horsekeeping programs.
- Help recycle good, solid horses from one owner to another or assist prospective new owners in locating sound, affordable, suitable, and safe horses. Stress the importance of prepurchase veterinary examinations. After the sale, try to retain new horse owners as satisfied clients by offering the quality services they need.
- Actively support youth riding programs, such as 4-H, Pony Club, and youth breed association activities. Recruit volunteer leaders to run or assist in the programs, or become a volunteer leader yourself.
- Subscribe to horse magazines, which will keep you up-to-date on the latest in teaching and training techniques, then donate them to schools or public libraries after you've read them. Suggest that other riding clubs or farms take the responsibility for doing this routinely in their areas.
- Promote the horse as a source of recreation, fun, and sport that benefits the physical and mental fitness of people of all ages. For instance, advertise and promote the horse in media that non–horse owners read, see, and use.
- Form a club specifically to promote horses. In Virginia, there is one called the Railsitters, which promotes horse racing and generates interest in the sport. Membership is open to all age groups and costs about $10 per year. For that price, members receive a newsletter, a membership card, and get discounts on special tours to horse farms, training facilities, and racetracks.
- Implement fun horse events that will attract and retain both the riding and nonriding public. Most people enjoy watching a jumper class. A drill team from one barn in Maryland rides in formation to music and puts on shows in conjunction with other events, such as summer crab feasts and holiday horse shows. It is always a hit with both riders and nonriders.
- Educate the public to the fact that people do *not* have to be wealthy to use and enjoy horses. Talk about alternatives to owning a horse outright, such as lease and shared-lease options.

$

Money-Saving Tip

Build your mailing list for free when you host events. Keep on hand a guest book with your name and logo on it. Put it in an accessible place and ask visitors to sign the book and provide their addresses. This increases the number of contacts on your mailing list.

Serve the Community

Participate in programs that permit disadvantaged families and families of average means to become involved with horses. Some stables have initiated an "Adopt a Pony" program; sponsors pay for the cost of the ponies, and inner-city youngsters come to ride them. Many horse farms have "labor for lessons" programs — students do barn work or groom horses in exchange for riding lessons. I think every child who wants to learn to ride should have the opportunity, and those of us in the horse industry can help make that happen.

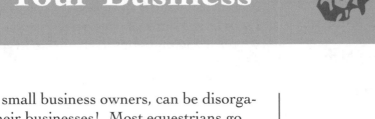

3
Managing Your Business

Horse people, like other small business owners, can be disorganized about running their businesses! Most equestrians go into the business because they know and love horses, not because they want to reconcile bank statements, organize files, or plan calendars. However, successfully managing your records and finances is instrumental in making a profit in this business.

I know how difficult it is to get and stay organized when it seems like you have so many other things going on. Several times I have taken checks from students in the middle of lessons and stuffed them in my dusty pocket, only to recover crumbled, illegible bits of paper from my washing machine a week later.

Lack of organization results in lost opportunities, lost time, and lost dollars. It takes time, planning, and diligence to create and maintain organization, but the process can be eased by following the advice in this section.

TIME MANAGEMENT

The horse business is long, hard work. It often requires putting in seven-day weeks and, if you have a colicky horse or a foaling mare, 24-hour days. Don't work harder; work smarter. Start by carefully planning your time.

Begin each morning by planning what you want to accomplish that day. Make a "to do" list and give each task a priority. If you have a list of 10 tasks that need to be accomplished, you may have two that are "A" priorities. Do those first. Don't fall victim to the "tyranny of the urgent." Let's say you schedule an important staff meeting for noon, and someone calls 15 minutes before the meeting and wants to come and look at a horse that day. Don't tell the potential customer to come at noon; have him come after the staff meeting. Stick with your priorities whenever possible.

Be sure to utilize idle time. For example, you can fit in phone calls or bookwork between classes at horse shows, or between customers while selling tack. (See Chapter 12 for information on opening a tack shop.)

There are many good tapes on time management and business management available at your local library or bookstore. Listen to them while you are driving to the feed store or hauling horses.

LABOR MANAGEMENT

Closely monitor the wages you pay for labor to make sure they don't exceed your budget. Careful planning can cut these costs drastically. **Install labor-saving devices**, such as automatic horse waterers, which cost about $30 each, or float-operated waterers, which cost about $10 apiece. (Remember, you are paying for labor every time a horse is watered.) In some parts of the country, catfish are placed in outdoor water tubs to keep tubs clean, further saving on labor costs. Consider this: If you have 60 horses in the barn:

    3 hours/day are spent watering
    3 hours x $5/hour wage = $15/day
    $15/day x 365 days a year = $5,475/year
    $5,475/year x 10 years = $54,750 spent in labor costs just
        for watering horses

Labor Management Cost-Savers

- **Establish cooperative programs** with agricultural schools. These programs often require a semester or more of work experience for students. You may provide room, board, or just a small stipend in exchange for their labor.

- **Establish work-study programs** for junior and senior high school students. Allow them to exchange work for lessons, leasing, or board. Closely supervise these programs and make adjustments as necessary.

- **Set clear responsibilities and schedules** for all employees so you don't have to spend time checking up on jobs and reminding people what they have to do. Your employees can work much more efficiently if they know horses are fed at 7:00 am and 5:00 pm, that stalls are cleaned by 10:30 am, and that horses are brought in from the pastures by 3:30 pm.

- **Practice good management;** it saves money as well as headaches. You can buy or borrow books on management that will give you other money-saving pointers.

STAFF INPUT

Regularly hold staff brainstorming sessions. Their input aids greatly in the planning process, and good communication is essential to being organized. Regular staff meetings not only keep everyone up on barn business, but they also give employees an opportunity to air grievances and contribute suggestions to resolve problems. Make sure employees feel they are heard. For instance, if instructors tell you that the dust is so bad in the rings that they and riding students are choking on it, investigate the possibility of installing a sprinkler system or set up a regular sprinkler schedule during dry seasons.

Next, set a date for a planning retreat. The most productive sessions are held off-grounds. Getting away will prevent distractions or interruptions from neighing horses, ringing phones, and talkative students. The getaway could be an elaborate weekend at a bed and breakfast or a breakfast meeting at a local fast-food restaurant.

As you begin planning, focus first on the big picture to avoid getting bogged down in details. Set short-term (six-month) and long-term (one-year, five-year, and ten-year) goals for your advertising, facilities, events/programs, horses, vehicles, and employees. Keep in mind that issues change, and these goals should be revisited and updated regularly.

ORGANIZATIONAL PLANNING

Planning ahead and organizing your business will help you achieve your goals. This outline will get you started.

I. Master Calendar
- Advertising calendar: when, where, and how much
- Budget
- Building and maintenance calendar: what needs to be built or repaired, and when it should be done
- Event/program calendar: lessons, horse shows, clinics, annual vaccinations, worming, Coggins tests, floating teeth
- Training and sales calendar: the number of weeks each horse needs to reach its optimum condition and obtain the maximum sale price; when to enter each horse in a show where it will do its best and gain high visibility; and an estimation of the date by which horses should be sold
- Vehicle maintenance calendar: repairs, tune-ups, new tires, and so forth. It is essential to keep current maintenance records on vehicles. Once I was told the farm

An umbrella canister is just one creative way to organize crops.

truck needed an entire new braking system. After checking the maintenance chart, I realized it had been done just 10 months earlier. I promptly took the truck to another mechanic, who agreed the brakes were fine. (See the Vehicle Maintenance Form in Appendix H, page 132.)

- Vehicle replacement calendar: when to sell older vehicles based on condition and depreciation, purchase new ones, and how much to start saving monthly toward new vehicles

II. Physical Organization Plan

- Post a list of contents on the inside doors of cabinets. This makes it easy to locate supplies and, if you note when an item is running low, you'll see at a glance when additional purchases need to be made.
- Paint your equipment with your farm colors to prevent others from mistaking it for their own and to keep equipment from getting lost or stolen at shows and events. Stencil your initials on buckets and tack boxes or wrap colored tape around the handles of pitchforks and brooms.
- Label exactly where equipment such as bridles and saddles should hang. To indicate where tools such as pitchforks and shovels go, outline their shape on the wall with spray paint. This reminds workers and students to return them to their proper place, and helps you spot missing tools and borrowed stable equipment.
- Assign a tidy person to be in charge of keeping the tack room organized. Well-maintained tack is vital to the smooth operation of your farm; when it is cleaned and hung properly, it lasts longer than if it is left scattered around the farm. Arrange the tack room so that visitors see the most organized section of the room; put dirty blankets or tack waiting to be cleaned in a less visible place.
- Be creative when organizing equipment. I used to waste time searching for crops and longe whips because there wasn't a designated place for them. I solved the problem by storing them in an umbrella canister.

III. Operational Organization

- Computers — modern-day timesavers — are discussed below. They are master organizers and timesavers, so if you don't have a computer now, seriously consider purchasing one. When talking to a salesperson, be clear about its intended uses so you come home with the right computer and software to help run your business.

- Use bulletin boards and chalkboards to communicate with employees and clients. Post important emergency phone numbers on a bulletin board next to the phone, and special feeding requests on a chalkboard near the feed bin.
- Create files on students, boarders, business associates, suppliers, veterinarians, farriers, and so on. (See the appendices for various forms you may want to keep on file.)
- Purchase other office-supply organizers such as Rolodexes, business-card holders, organizational trays, and filing cabinets that you need to organize your business.
- Keep charts to help you and the staff track breeding, exercise, feeding, and shoeing schedules for your horses. (See Shoeing Chart in Appendix B, page 126.)

List the contents on the inside door of cabinets. This makes it easy to determine what supplies are missing at a glance.

Ross Chapple

A neatly organized tack room encourages students to keep tack clean and in place.

- Once a year, conduct a complete inventory of all equipment, facilities, tack, supplies, horses, employees, programs, and vehicles. Evaluate what should stay, what should go, what's missing, and what needs to be replaced.

IV. Personnel Organization

Establish a schedule for meeting with each staff member privately and with the staff as a group. Discuss as appropriate:
- Employee reviews
- Hiring, firing, and training needs
- Instructor skill reviews
- Raises and promotions

Once you begin this process, you may recognize additional areas that could be organized more efficiently. Review the Organization Calendar in Appendix J, page 138.

INSURANCE

Insurance is integral to good business planning. It's a necessary expense; without it, losses and liabilities could destroy everything you've worked to accomplish.

Health Insurance

Providing health insurance to employees, even if you can only afford to pay a portion of the premium, is an excellent way to attract and retain good workers. Employees with access to health care are likelier to stay healthy, which means fewer lost days of work and a more productive performance when they are at work.

If you decide to provide health insurance, shop among several insurers for the best premium on coverage that meets the needs of your employees. The least expensive insurance tends to be a group insurance policy with a high deductible. Ask if the plan you are considering contracts with hospitals convenient to the farm, and if most employees will be able to continue using their own physicians.

Horse Insurance

Two primary types of insurance for horses are mortality insurance and major medical coverage. If you could not afford to replace a horse if something happened to it, then mortality insurance is probably a good idea. Insurance can be very expensive and offer extremely limited coverage, so, when weighing this decision, be sure to ask specifically what causes of injury or death are included.

Major medical coverage is another type of insurance to consider. Policies differ, but according to one equine insurance agent, coverage is usually limited to $5,000 per animal per year, and there is often a $250 deductible per incident or illness. Major medical would provide coverage for necessary surgical procedures, such as colic surgery. In addition, it would help cover expenses for other costly medical problems, such as Potomac fever, or a lameness problem such as founder, once they exceed $250. To obtain major medical coverage, you may have to buy mortality coverage as part of the package.

There are some common restrictions on insurance policies covering horses. Many companies will not insure a horse over age 15 for major medical events, although it is possible to obtain mortality coverage for older horses. Coverage for preexisting conditions is also likely to be excluded. If a horse requiring colic surgery has to have an intestinal resection, you will find that most insurers will not insure that horse for colic in the future. If a horse has a bout with colic that requires only nonsurgical medical treatment, or undergoes colic surgery but did not require a resection, coverage for colic will be removed from the policy; once the horse is colic-free for one year, coverage for colic may again be restored.

Another type of horse insurance is for loss of use. Again, the specifics will vary with the policy, but here's an example of how this coverage can work: You insure a valuable jumper under a policy that covers the horse specifically for this use. The horse then sustains a permanent injury. The insurer would pay the owner 50 percent of the insured amount and the horse would remain with the owner. Or the insurer would pay the owner 75 percent of the insured amount and take possession of the horse. Under such contracts, insurers have the right to have the horse destroyed, but usually will try to sell the horse for some other use, perhaps as a companion or trail horse. To purchase loss of use coverage, you must purchase mortality and major medical coverage.

Certainly, insuring horses against mortality and major medical bills is expensive, but it may be a good investment if you have a major medical event. It can be comforting to know you would be able to cover the bill and provide the treatment. Sometimes insurance is not worth the money. It certainly is not if you have 10 school horses and the premiums will cost more than it would cost you to replace them. It may be a better business decision to take a loss or two rather than pay premiums to cover these animals.

Tips For Insuring Horses

If you want to insure your horses, there are several ways to keep costs to a minimum:

- Shop around for the best premium. Do not, however, sacrifice quality service, such as prompt claims payment, for a lower premium.

- If your premium is sizable, find out if you can arrange for a payment plan with a minimal or no service charge.

- If you need to insure a large number of horses, inquire about getting a discount for insuring them all through the same company.

- Ask other horse owners which agents and insurance companies they have found that provide the most competitive rates and best claims services.

Property Insurance

Property insurance is vital to your business. Consult with an agent experienced in dealing with farm properties. Make sure your insurance will cover equipment, such as tack, when you are transporting it to shows.

Keep a list of everything your policy covers and its estimated value. Some insurance companies recommend photographing or videotaping insured items to supplement your records; if your policy covers equipment in your tack room, for example, film the tack room when all the equipment is in place.

Liability Insurance

If you keep horses primarily for pleasure, some coverage may be included as part of your property insurance. For any type of horse business, however, liability insurance is crucial, and in some states it is mandatory, and may have to be purchased in addition to property insurance. The skyrocketing cost of liability insurance has made operating a horseback-riding stable far more expensive than it used to be. However, there are ways to help keep down premiums — and minimize the likelihood of getting sued:

- Require riders or parents to sign release forms before you let students mount a horse. Contact a local attorney to obtain the appropriate forms.
- Require all riders to wear helmets that meet ASTM/SEI safety standards, and boots or shoes with heels.
- Hire only safety-conscious, qualified instructors.
- Teach with sound and safe horses.
- Check with your state horse organizations to see if they offer any group policies.
- Practice safety in and around the barn and on the horse at all times. Stop and correct any practices that are unsafe. It is your responsibility to teach students the proper way to tack up, lead, mount, and dismount a horse. You will also want to teach etiquette and safety on trail rides and when riding in a ring with more than one horse.
- If anyone even hints that he may have a liability claim against your stable, check out the source of the claim. At a stable where I once worked, a couple came for a trail ride, fell off their horses, and said they were injured. Then they tried to sue for damages. Mysteriously, their release forms had disappeared. Suspecting foul play, we checked around with other stables and found out this was not the couple's first "accident." In other cases, they also sued, and received

Safety equipment can reduce injuries. Require that all riders wear helmets that meet ASTM/SEI safety standards and sturdy boots with heels.

out-of-court settlements. In the case of the stable where I worked, we insisted upon going to trial. We had large attorney's fees, but we won — and had the satisfaction of knowing that this couple did not get away with a fraudulent claim against our stable.

Make sure your agent understands all the various activities that go on at your farm to ensure that you obtain all the types of insurance coverage you need.

INTEGRATED SYSTEMS

Integrating the various services you provide, such as schooling, boarding, and breeding, will enable you to make the most of your horses from birth to retirement or for however long you are associated with any horse you handle.

Let's say that you breed your mare to a very handsome Conformation Hunter Stallion. Eleven months later she foals and you're the proud owner of Royal Ruth, a pretty gray filly. When she's ready for halter-breaking, you set up a short course on how to halter-break a foal. Seven students take the course and not only do you take in their course fees, but Royal Ruth is now halter-broken.

As Royal Ruth matures, you can offer similar instruction on how to train a horse to longe and break to saddle. Royal Ruth impresses one of your advanced students, Laura. You make arrangements to lease Royal Ruth to Laura, who is now paying for

Make the most of each horse in your barn.

Breed Mare, Raise Foal

Give Halter-Breaking Demo

Have Student Train Foal

Use Horse for Lessons

Lease Horse to Student

Sell Horse to Student

Sell Saddle to New Owner

Receive Board from New Owner

leasing as well as lessons. When Royal Ruth is ready to show, you can receive the trailering fee and the horse show schooling fee. Since Laura is paying her own entry fees, Royal Ruth is basically being shown for you free of charge. You would only want to trust a young horse to a capable, experienced rider and handler under your supervision.

Later, Laura moves out of town, and Katie, another student, expresses interest in buying Royal Ruth. Your selling price is more than she can afford so you reduce the price to encourage Katie to buy the horse and keep her on your farm, where you can continue to profit from the animal. The mare is now a proven show horse; Katie boards her at your barn, continues to take lessons from you, and goes to shows with you.

For Christmas, Katie's parents buy her a new saddle and bridle from your tack shop. Her mom decides to take lessons so that she can start riding the horse as well. Now you are receiving board payments, lesson fees, and tack sales from your horse sale.

A few years later, Katie is off to college and wants you to sell the horse for her. Because of Royal Ruth's excellent training and show record, which Katie paid for, the horse's value is quite high. You sell Royal Ruth to Brant, a rider who is new in the area, and you receive a sales commission. He is busy with his job so you offer full board services including grooming, clipping, and exercising. Now you can increase your profits by offering more services, in addition to regular board fees. Brant also needs the mare exercised so you offer to use her in the riding school. A cost-free school horse is now available for your riding program.

After some years, Brant decides to breed Royal Ruth.

Eleven months later you have a new boarder horse to train and break. The process begins again. After many years of useful service, Royal Ruth retires on your farm, with Brant paying for pasture board for the rest of her days.

This is what I mean by an integrated system. By planning ahead and taking advantage of opportunities, you can get significant mileage out of each and every horse.

4
Financial Management

The first step in proper financial management is to set goals. Carefully consider your financial expectations. Whether you aim to earn your living from a horse business or simply to minimize the costs of a primarily recreational endeavor, set clear goals first and then work toward those goals in a systematic way for the best results.

Simple financial techniques can help you implement your goals and monitor your progress. If you cringe over such terms as "budgets" and "financial models," take heart; it is not as difficult as you may think. Careful planning and monitoring helps to ensure that your horse business at least breaks even or, preferably, turns a profit.

DEVISING A BUDGET

To manage your horse activities well, you need a realistic budget to help you monitor your ongoing operations and to assist you in making important business decisions.

If you are unfamiliar with budgeting, just think of it as a record-keeping file cabinet all on one piece of paper. It enables you to track expenses and receipts. Remember that a budget is more than just a one-time plan for revenues and expenses; it is a *system* for continuous financial record keeping and a method of comparing actual results with anticipated results. For instance, if you want to enter the horse boarding business, you'll need to come up with a profitable rate to charge boarders.

Starting and maintaining a budget takes time and discipline, but it yields information that gives you freedom and power over your finances, instead of the other way around. Fortunately, the advent of relatively low-cost personal computers and software has made it easier than ever before for a dedicated equestrian to become a part-time financial whiz. At the very least, it can keep you from dreading budgeting as you would a root canal.

Budgeting will give you freedom and power over your finances, instead of the other way around!

In Appendix K (page 140),
you will find a sample budget that includes an income statement and a cash-flow statement for a hypothetical horse operation. There are blank forms for your use that can be adjusted for your type and scale of operation. Although forms themselves are helpful, the most effective way to build and monitor a budget forecast is to create a flexible financial model using available computer software, assuming you have a personal computer. Find a model that enables you to expand easily on the type of information you want to track. Consider a software package that also will assist you with budgeting, tax planning, and banking. With that help, you can assess your current financial performance or run an analysis to determine just how your profits are affected by changes in costs, pricing of services, and the addition or removal of certain activities. As with most financial issues, consult with an accountant or a business consultant to help you set up your system. You will save time and money if your model is set up to make extracting tax information easier.

You should be especially aware of two primary formats used in budgeting: the income statement and the cash-flow statement.

THE INCOME STATEMENT

The income statement is a tool that helps you assess the overall profitability of your operation and, if presented in sufficient

♘ *You should be aware of two primary formats used in budgeting: the income statement and the cash-flow statement.*

detail, determines the viability of individual parts of your business. Your goal should be to develop a system that budgets, tracks, and segregates the separate categories of both revenue and expense. In the example in Appendix K, page 140, we look at 18 different possible sources of revenue (perhaps you can develop more) and track 21 categories of expenses (perhaps you can develop fewer)!

Fixed and Variable Costs

After you have identified various expenses, it is important to group them into at least the two major categories known as fixed costs and variable costs. **Fixed costs** (overhead costs) are constant over the period of your budget and do not vary or change as activity levels change. The cost of leasing property or your mortgage payment would be a fixed cost. **Variable costs** are those that change with the level of business. This would include the costs of goods sold by your barn as this will change directly in proportion with the amount of goods sold.

The delineation of fixed and variable costs is a useful concept when analyzing financial results. It helps identify possible earning problems. It can tell you whether or not you have what is known as a negative gross profit (net sales minus variable costs), which means you are losing money even *before* you incur your fixed costs. Once you recognize these problems, you can begin finding ways to solve them. You may need to charge more for the services you provide and reduce variable expenses.

Information provided by the income statement also can help prevent you from inadvertently *increasing* your losses by expanding unprofitable segments of your business. Let's say that overall your horse operation is profitable. You decide to increase profits by doubling the amount of business you do. However, if you haven't broken down the operation to see which parts of the business are profitable and which aren't, you could end up losing money. Say that riding lessons, analyzed as one activity, turn a profit. Boarding actually results in a loss of $10 a horse per month. If you double the number of boarders, you'll double your losses. This analysis of your business tells you that you need to charge more for boarding whether or not you choose to expand it.

If expenses are getting out of hand, it is usually easier to find ways to reduce variable costs in the short run than it is to reduce fixed costs.

If fixed costs prove to be your main impediment to earning a profit, then either you will need to significantly increase the total level of your sales and services, such as boarding, to cover your overhead, or it may be best to scale back overhead costs while trying to maintain the same level of business. You could accomplish this by selling fixed assets, moving to a site with facilities that are more appropriate for the size of your business, or even laying off administrative or other staff who do not directly contribute to earnings.

Common Sizing

As shown in the Summary Income Statement on the next page, it can be very useful to look at your income statement in a "common-sized" format, which simply shows various activities as a percentage of your total revenue. This approach helps you to measure the relative as well as the actual contribution of each aspect of your business to profits or costs. Just a glance at the percentages shown on a common-sized financial statement can often help you quickly identify activities that contribute to or detract from profits. For a simple example of how to utilize information from a very basic common-sized income statement, let's look at Harry's Horse Farm.

The first thing the income statement tells Harry is the good news that he made a $200 gross profit (total revenue minus variable costs) in 1997 and $100 in net income from sales of $1,000. The common-sized results point out further that Harry earned a 20% gross profit margin (gross profit as a percentage of total revenue) and that he made a 10% net profit margin (net income as a percentage of total revenue). He can use this percentage to compare with other horse operations of any size or to compare to his own prior year or future years' results to tell him how he may be improving at making income out of revenue. Harry might be happy having earned a profit, but he can learn much more from his budget results if he just takes a closer look.

Harry will discover some surprising things from his income statement, including the fact that his major revenue source actually makes no money at all. Riding lessons break even for Harry (the revenue and expenses related to lessons are both 43% of total revenue and net each other out). Expanding his riding lesson business alone will be a wasted effort unless he can charge more or spend less in the process.

Now, look at tack sales. Although they make up 27% of total revenue, the cost of tack is only 6% of total revenue; thus, tack sales are the most profitable line of business for Harry. Whether he realized it or not, Harry is really in the retail tack business, and giving lessons is not a direct moneymaker. Until he can improve his gross profit for lessons, teaching will simply remain a tool for bringing the customers to his tack store and not the other way around. While he may love teaching infinitely more than selling tack, he now understands that tack butters his bread over 1,000% more than lessons do!

Finally, Harry should note that while selling Old Red generated 30% of his revenue, he actually lost money on the sale because the cost of Red was greater than the sale price. Had Harry not maintained accurate records, he might never have realized that the sale of Red brought about a loss. So along with expanding his tack business and reducing what it costs him to give lessons, perhaps by using boarder horses, the numbers also remind Harry that he should continue to keep good records.

While Harry has learned a great deal about his business from his income statement, he has at least one more thing to do before making any final budget decisions. Harry should take a look at his cash-flow statement, which provides some different and very useful information.

HARRY'S HORSE FARM

SUMMARY INCOME STATEMENT FOR 1997

Revenue		% of total Revenue
Riding lessons	$ 433	43%
Tack sales	271	27%
Sale of Old Red	296	30%
Total revenue	$1,000	100%
Expenses - Variable		
Riding lesson expenses	$433	43%
Cost of tack sales	57	6%
Cost of Old Red	310	31%
Total variable expenses	$800	80%
Gross profit	$200	20%
Expenses - Fixed		
Depreciation	$20	2%
Interest on loan	50	5%
Total fixed expenses	$70	7%
Total expenses	$870	87%
Pre-tax income	$130	13%
Income tax	30	3%
Net income	$100	10%

THE CASH-FLOW STATEMENT

Where does all the money go? Will I have sufficient cash this year to carry out my plans? A cash-flow statement can answer some of these basic questions.

The cash-flow statement adjusts the income statement for any non-cash income statement items, such as depreciation, which are important for your tax calculation but are not so important for your day-to-day cash management. It also measures those changes in assets and liabilities that do not affect income, but certainly do affect cash and, thus, your day-to-day ability to keep operating.

It is imperative that you understand the difference between cash flow and income. What most people don't realize is that a successful, growing business can easily run out of cash, even if it's making a profit. How? The earnings are being reinvested in the assets needed to grow the business. A successful business can go bankrupt if, when planning for cash, you do not provide the resources needed to pay creditors on a timely basis.

An example of how a cash-flow crunch can occur during a profitable year can be found in the breeding business. If you agree to offer credit terms on the stud fees to the mare owners (deferring payment until later in the year), you may be short on cash to pay for feed and labor costs associated with the mare's care during the breeding season. Since your employees want to be paid on time, you don't have the option of asking them to defer their paychecks just because the stud fees haven't arrived yet. A solution might be to have the mare's owner pay board and veterinary fees when the service is rendered and reserve the stud fee for the final payment. Just be sure to take the timing of cash flow into consideration in addition to profitability when planning your yearly budget.

Let's consider Harry's Horse Farm again to focus further on this topic of cash-flow management. The following cash-flow statement demonstrates that Harry's 1997 results were actually a $30 *drain* on cash even though he made a $100 profit.

While the tack shop may represent Harry's most profitable business, he will need to be careful how rapidly he grows that business because it will require buying more inventory for his tack shop — and this initially will eat up more cash than it will bring in. Also, unless he is careful not to sell on credit terms, the bills he is owed by customers (receivables) will grow more rapidly than the cash he is receiving. As his business stabilizes, the growth in the amount of receivables and inventory will cease to be a problem *but as long as he grows his business,* more cash will be locked up in activities like buying new saddles and giving credit terms to customers than in deposits to his bank account. In the cash-flow statement,

♘ Examples of items that do not change income but do affect cash flow are changes in receivables (payments owed to you for sales made on credit) and changes in inventory. Two other important items are purchases or sales of fixed assets (such as a truck or land) and payment of principal on loans.

you can see that the growth of receivables ($200) and inventory ($100) drained $300 in cash from Harry.

Back in the Income Statement section we gave Harry a little grief for selling Old Red at a small loss. Certainly, Harry cannot base his business over the long term solely on selling horses at a loss. However, *from a cash-flow perspective* the sale of Old Red (even below cost) could well have been the right thing to do. The sale of Old Red brought in to the business much-needed cash, which in turn can now be invested in more tack shop inventory to help that more profitable business grow. It could also be used to reduce the loan on his farm, thereby further reducing his fixed costs over the long term. We learn from the cash-flow statement that because of the negative $180 "net cash after operations," Harry had to reduce his fixed assets further by selling an old bushhog mower for $200 at cost to raise more cash. We also learn that Harry had to make a $50 payment on his land loan; because it is not an expense — but a reduction of a liability — it was not reflected in the income statement. Hopefully, Harry has learned the value of using a cash flow statement, as well as an income statement in the future management of his farm!

In summary, you need an income statement both to measure the long-term profitability of your overall business and to assess the viability of the various revenue-earning activities. Also, looking at the common-sized income statement on a percentage-of-revenue

The careful monitoring and planning of cash movements helps a profitable business avoid becoming a cash-poor one.

HARRY'S HORSE FARM

SUMMARY CASH-FLOW STATEMENT FOR 1997

Total Revenue	$1,000	
– increase in accounts receivable *	200	
Total cash collected from operations		800
– total expenses (including income tax, not depreciation)	$880	
– increase in tack shop inventory	100	
Net cash after operations		($180)**
– Loan payment on land	50	
+ Sale of bushhog mower	200	
Net Cash Flow		($30)

* sales allowing deferred payment

** note: ( ) indicates negative number

A partial budget is a simple, but very useful, four-step process to help you think through whether a new business idea will be a contributor to a total profit.

basis helps make all these issues clearer. Finally, be cognizant of your cash position by utilizing a cash-flow statement so you can avoid a short-term cash crisis while growing those parts of your business that your income statement indicates are worth growing. The careful monitoring and planning of cash movements helps a profitable business avoid becoming a cash-poor one. (Appendix K, page 140, contains an example of a cash-flow statement that demonstrates how cash flow can also be greater than net income. It also contains a blank cash-flow form as a sample.)

PARTIAL BUDGET FOR TESTING NEW IDEAS

Many of the ideas in this book will result in profitable additions or useful changes to your current horse operation. But how do you know if a given idea is suitable for your particular situation? What may be a moneymaker for one operation on the East Coast may not be profitable on the Pacific coast. How can you know what new lines of business or changes in practice will truly help your unique situation? A partial budget is the answer. It involves what I call *organized brainstorming* as you consider (1) added revenues expected; (2) reduced costs, if any, as compared to your current practice; (3) reductions in revenue that could occur; and (4) any added costs to expect. Finally, you bring these factors together and make an informed decision. (See the sample partial budget form in Appendix K on page 140.) You may wish to draw up several partial budget versions for the same proposed activity using different assumptions to decide whether that new business activity would be viable under multiple scenarios of cost and revenue. If you still net a profit or are willing to sustain a loss for a year or two until that part of the business takes off, then you probably have an idea that is ready to work for you. A simplified example of how to use this budget appears on the facing page.

TAX WRITE-OFFS

If you use some of the ideas in this book, you will be more aware of the moneymaking areas of your business and be able to turn a profit. The Internal Revenue Service (IRS) requires business owners to show a profit two out of five years. Otherwise, it may consider the business a hobby, and deductions could be disallowed.

Successful businesses are entitled to many deductions, and you'll want to take advantage of every one you can. Traditionally, donating horses to universities, police departments, and therapeutic riding centers provides tax write-offs for horse businesses. We had

Partial Budget

The new service or activity being considered:
2-week Christmas camp held weekdays from 9 am – 4 pm

1) ADDED RECEIPTS:

(This is added income from the new service, which would include the fee charged for the number of camp students anticipated, after-camp child care, etc.).

Tuition for 20 children at $250 each $5,000
After-camp care 4–6 pm for 10 children at $5 an hour $1,000

Total $6,000

2) REDUCED COSTS:

(Any costs that might be reduced by the addition of a new service. If you initiate a Christmas camp, for instance, you might give regular barn staff a two-week vacation and have camp counselors take over the feeding of horses.)

3 employees earning $6 an hour @ 40 hours per week $1,440

Total $1,440

(A) Added receipts plus reduced costs $7,440

3) REDUCED RECEIPTS:

(This would be any lost income that occurs as a result of a Christmas camp. You might, for instance, eliminate weekday riding lessons during the camp because you need the horses for Christmas camp students; thus you would lose income paid by your usual weekday students.)

10 weekday students at $25 each per week $500

Total $500

4) ADDED COSTS:

(With the Christmas camp, you will have added costs such as salaries for camp instructors and counselors.)

Two additional instructors/counselors to supplement existing
instructor staff at $20 an hour for seven hours daily $2,800
Two instructors for after-camp care 4 pm–6pm at $10 hour. $400

Total $3,200

(B) Reduced receipts plus added costs $3,700

(C) Net difference to the new service or activity
Subtract Line B from Line A) $3,740

a Quarter horse mare that bowed a tendon. We could not use her in the riding school, so we donated her to Texas A&M's veterinary school. It was beneficial to the students' education, the mare was well taken care of, and it was a nice tax write-off and a good business decision for us.

Tax laws change, however, so hire an accountant who is knowledgeable about the laws affecting the horse industry. Ask other horse owners to recommend an accountant.

Information on tax laws affecting the horse industry also are available from the American Horse Council. (See Appendix L, page 146, for the address.)

BARTERING

The barter or trading of goods or services eliminates the need for exchanging money. When services or products of equal value are bartered, you don't have to have the cash up front to pay for them. Bartering also eliminates the need to pay sales tax if products of equal value are exchanged. If you trade a $3,000 horse for a $3,000 trailer, and the sales tax is 5%, you'll save $150.

When bartering, however, IRS requirements must again be adhered to. According to one accountant, if your business is ever audited, there are two questions the IRS agent is likely to ask: Did you have income you did not report to the IRS and did you have any bartering transactions? The IRS requires you to report the value of goods and services received; you may be able to deduct what you gave in exchange if it is a business expense, but probably not if it is a personal expense. Track bartering transactions and the value of each transaction, and present them to your accountant.

Before you start bartering, make a list of your products and services. Then think of people with businesses that offer products or services you need. Get on the phone and locate those interested in bartering for lessons, boarding, and so forth. Here are some suggestions:

Offered	Needed
camp	building materials or fencing
trailering	feed
tack	farrier
board	printing, paper
aged manure	bedding
training	veterinary, legal, medical
consulting	services
lessons	advertising
	repairs, carpentry

COMPUTERS AND SOFTWARE

In today's fast-paced, information-filled world, computers are becoming as essential on farms as pitchforks. Computers can save time and money by helping you better organize your business and maintain records more easily. There are several inexpensive farm management software programs available. Check with your local computer store for recommendations.

If you're not comfortable with computers, take an introductory computer course, or see if local computer stores offer free lessons when you buy merchandise from them. Computer manuals are often difficult for the novice to understand; however, most computer packges have tutorials to familiarize you with the system. Here is just some of the important information you can store and maintain on your computer:

- Employee records
- Mailing lists that can be alphabetized, updated, and printed as address labels
- Budget plans, cash-flow statements, and general accounting figures
- Horse show management, including entries, payments, points, prize lists, adds/scratches, refunds, class results, championship and reserve championship calculations, and master sheets
- Horse records, such as age, veterinary and farrier schedules, and so forth.
- Tax records
- Billings
- Checking accounts
- Graphics for farm brochures, camp certificates, and advertisements

With relatively inexpensive personal computers and software, sound financial management is at your fingertips. (It's also easier and more interesting than you might think.) Even if you hire an accountant or convince your spouse to take on responsibility for the day-to-day finances, you'll still need to familiarize yourself with the budgeting process and understand your monthly and annual financial statements.

Extra Management Tips
- Develop a financial forecast using a simple computer model and keep up-to-date financial records. Analyze the resulting income statements to help you to make wise management decisions.

⊍ It's probably not a good idea to penalize boarders and students who usually pay promptly and, for one reason or another, pay late once or even twice. But you'll want to be able to collect a late charge from clients who are chronically delinquent with payment, and to charge for returned checks.

- Complete and assess your cash-flow statement monthly.
- Require written boarding, leasing, lesson, and sales contracts. With the help of your attorney, design standard forms to keep on hand, and get all transactions in writing. (Some of the forms you'll need appear in the Appendices.)
- Establish a tax file and keep all receipts for your accountant.
- Open an interest-bearing, free-checking account.
- Establish a savings and retirement plan for yourself.
- Send out bills promptly. Give yourself the option of charging interest, such as 1.5% monthly, for outstanding balances.
- Turn seriously delinquent accounts over to a collection agency. Include a clause in your boarding agreement allowing you to sell a horse if board is unpaid for three consecutive months.
- Pay your own bills on time to avoid interest or penalty payments, but don't pay any earlier than you must. Have the money in an account that bears interest, which can really add up. The exception might be companies that give discounts for paying bills early; in such cases, weigh the cost of the discount against the interest you get from your bank account, then decide whether it is more profitable to pay the bill early or on time.
- Require all payments for services in advance. Ask boarders to pay their board for June by June 1. Ask students to pay for lessons ahead of time, too, which helps ensure they'll show up for each scheduled class. One way to do this is by selling a group of five or 10 lessons at a slight discount, so the students commit to and pay for these in advance. Plan lesson blocks quarterly instead of monthly to reduce the number of bills you send out and the money you spend on postage.

5
Riding Programs, Boarding, and Leasing

Horseback riding lessons and boarding horses are the mainstays of many horse businesses. You may choose to do one or the other but, if you do both, the potential for making money may be far greater.

RIDING SCHOOLS

Offering riding lessons to the public can be enjoyable for you as well as for your students. It's gratifying to teach riders of all ages and levels safety measures and the proper care of horses, and to impart your own philosophy and love for these animals. There are three important components that will make your riding school profitable as well:
- Qualified instructors
- Reliable school horses
- Organized scheduling

Instructors

Find instructors interested in teaching all levels of riding. Some instructors scoff at teaching beginners, and some barns don't even offer beginner lessons. They may not realize that they're losing tremendous profit potential, since many of those beginners would be the dedicated students and boarders of the future.

Strive to find instructors sensitive to the needs of anyone interested in horses. Lessons should be educational and fun, particularly for beginners and children. Adults, of course, will need lessons planned for their level of maturity.

It is important that instructors have a plan for each lesson and short-term and long-range goals for their students. Telling students day after day to keep their heels down and their eyes up can get boring for instructors and students. Have a variety of teaching tools in your mental toolbox, and a somewhat uniform curriculum. Remember to provide guidance for substitute instructors. There

Be sure to carefully demonstrate the basics like grooming, bridling, and saddling.

Cynthia McFarland

☙ **Qualified instructors must have not only knowledge and experience with horses and riding, but also the patience and communication skills necessary to pass proper skills on to students with varying levels of ability.**

are many books available that give ideas for classes. An example is *101 Arena Exercises* by Cherry Hill. Send instructors to an instructor clinic. Watch videos together to find fresh teaching ideas and keep your staff interested.

When beginning students are around, there should be ample staff to help them handle the horses. New riders obviously want to be around horses, but can be intimidated until they learn just how to work with the animals, which may take weeks or even months of lessons.

For many of these early lessons, have students pair up. Here is a suggested curriculum for beginners during the first several classes:

- Show the facility, from the tack room to the bathroom.
- Demonstrate how to groom, pick feet, bridle, saddle up, and lead the horse.
- Practice proper mounting and dismounting.
- Have students work in pairs to lead each other on the horse, while the instructor teaches the proper position and basic aids, such as halting.
- Teach students how to untack horses and put away tack properly.

School Horses

School horses are the bread and butter of a riding school. Therefore, their selection, care, and training are of tremendous importance. The least expensive horses to use are the ones you don't own or pay to maintain. To reduce expenses, ask if any boarders in the barn would let you use their horses for lessons in exchange for a reduced board bill or a few free lessons. Often, it can be a welcome arrangement for boarders, who want their horses to get regular exercise but don't have the time to provide it themselves. It's especially helpful to "borrow" horses instead of buying them when you need them for a short period of time, such as during camps.

When you do buy horses, keep in mind that certain types are less expensive to maintain, particularly over the long haul. For instance, a short, stocky grade horse tends to be an easy keeper and is more likely to stay sound lesson after lesson. This saves money compared with a Thoroughbred, which can be more expensive to feed. Ponies are less expensive to purchase and maintain than are horses and may not need shoes. Obviously, you need a few big

A short, stocky grade horse may be easier and less costly to keep than bigger, expensive horses.

horses around to teach the older and taller students and a few "fancy" school horses to take to shows. But overall, particularly for beginner and intermediate riders, the horses don't have to be large, attractive, or expensive.

Every year, reevaluate your string of horses and identify those that are proving to be a problem. Some just need time off; others should be sold. I have a rule with school horses: three strikes and they're out, no matter how good they are on a day-to-day basis. If a certain horse kicks another horse during a lesson, a month later throws a rider, and then, a few weeks later, bites someone, he gets sold. Even if the horse is an excellent one for beginners most of the time, the harm he could cause on the occasional times he's bad is not worth the risk.

Beginner horses must be unflappable. Beginning riders are your best long-range source of income, assuming they are happy and continue to move up to the next level and start showing. They need a dependable horse they can trust to build up their confidence.

Take good care of school horses. This is essential if you want them to serve you well and maintain a good reputation for your barn. This includes making sure they are routinely inoculated, shod, and fed properly. Sick, lame, or thin horses always cost more to nurse than horses properly maintained along the way. You also are likely to bring in more business if your horses are healthy-looking and clean instead of thin and dirty.

Train school horses for the appropriate level and type of riding. And instead of training a horse to be used in the jumping classes yourself, get one of your advanced students to do it. Either have her lease the horse until it is ready to go into the school or, under your supervision, let the student take lessons and train it during lessons. Not only does this get the horse trained, but it also gives the student the valuable opportunity to learn how to train a horse and see its progress.

Group lessons pay the highest dividends per hour.

© June Campbell

Periodically "tune up" school horses. Even the best of them can get a little disobedient or confused because of incorrect signals naturally given by beginners. Have your advanced students ride the beginner horses for a lesson and have them perform various obedience drills. This will teach the students how to reschool horses and it will get the horse back on track.

Organizing Lessons

Organization is key to a successful riding program. Here are some pointers for scheduling and reducing paperwork.

- Reduce the amount of paperwork by offering lessons in quarterly sessions instead of weekly or monthly. For example:

    Fall session: September through December
    Christmas Break Camp
    Spring session: January through May
    Summer Session: June through August
    Summer Day Camp: (Two-week sessions require
        less paperwork than one-week sessions)

- Keep all medical records and release forms on file so you don't waste paper and time refiling new forms for the same students every session. (See the Student Record Form in Appendix D, page 128.)

After-School Lessons

Obviously, weekends and after school are prime times for students to take lessons. Organize your schedule to fit in as many lessons as possible after 3 pm on weekdays. Students should learn how to groom and tack up their own horses and to untack them and put them away. However, if time is short, have your staff groom and tack up the horses in advance.

⚘ Have students pay for the entire session, or at least half the session, in advance. Give a discount if they pay for the entire session up front. You'll have fewer bills to send out, and you collect interest on the money received in advance.

SAMPLE SCHEDULE

3:30–4 pm Students arrive, groom, and tack up.
4–4:50 pm Lesson
5–5:50 pm Second group of lessons
    After the students are finished, they return the horses to their stalls, loosen the girths, and remove the bridles and hang them outside the stalls.
6:15 pm Adult students coming from work arrive, put bridles on, tighten up the girths.
6:30–7:20 pm Lesson
    Students return the horses to their stalls and untack them.

During fall and winter sessions, you may only have two hours of daylight after school to teach, say 3:30–5:30 pm. The horses can already be tacked up for the first set of students, who ride 3:30–4:20 pm. The next set of students can ride the same horses 4:30–5:20 pm. These students can untack the horses. Note: You may find it a worthwhile investment to install lights to allow for later lessons during winter months.

LESSON POSSIBILITIES	
One-hour group lesson with seven students in a class	@ $25/student = $175
Semiprivate lesson with two students	@ $35 = $70
Private one-hour lesson with one student	@ $55
One half-hour private lesson	@ $30

Obviously, the group lesson pays the highest dividend per one hour of your time. So, you should not offer private instruction when you could be holding a group lesson. Private lessons are, however, good moneymakers to fill in gaps between group lessons.

Prepare a daily chart of riders and their horse assignments. Students check off their names; the instructors double-check the list for accuracy. Record this on your master chart or computer so that you can accurately track makeups and cancellations.

Cancellation/Makeup Policy

Generally, make it your policy to teach rain or shine. You might establish a policy that the stable shuts down only when schools are closed due to hazardous weather.

When the stable is open but the weather is too severe to teach outside and you don't have an indoor ring, prepare an interesting ground lesson. This is less time-consuming than calling all students to cancel a lesson because of the weather or to have 50 mothers calling in to see if you are teaching.

Limit the number of lessons that students can miss and then make up. Require that they cancel at least 24 hours before their lesson so that, if possible, you can find someone to take their place. If they cancel their makeup lesson, offer no further makeups.

Video Cameras

A video camera is an excellent training tool. Record a class session and let your students actually see when their heels aren't down or when they duck to the side over a fence.

USE VIDEOS AS A SALES TOOL

Videos also can be used to sell horses. Send them to potential out-of-state clients who might not drive all the way to your farm. Charge a refundable deposit so you get your tape back.

Videotaping courses and flat classes at horse shows can be a financial opportunity. Set up a booth at the shows where competitors can sign up and pay to have their classes videotaped. After the class, let them view or buy the tape. (See the Video Order Form in Appendix G, page 131.) The same can be done with still photography as well.

THERAPEUTIC RIDING PROGRAMS

Horseback riding lessons for those with disabilities can be a wonderful therapeutic experience. Riding builds motor skills and confidence for the students, gives great joy to instructors and volunteers, and provides good public relations for the barn.

Depending on the degree of the disability, you may need special equipment, such as a wheelchair ramp, stirrup covers, and hand-hold and safety straps, but the main ingredients for a successful experience are unflappable horses and plenty of volunteers (usually three per rider).

In some areas, you can set up a program with city parks and recreation agencies. They provide professionals with expertise in

Offering riding lessons for the disabled is rewarding for you and is good public relations for your barn.

Equus Therapeutic

working with people with disabilities, and you provide the equestrian teaching knowledge. At one ranch where I worked, we won a mayor's award for meritorious service for our therapeutic riding program. We received publicity, and a plaque that impressed visitors. Many of the volunteers and parents of students in the program later took lessons.

For more information, contact the Cheff Center (see Appendix L, page 146).

GENERAL SAFETY

Horseback riding can be a dangerous sport; falling off of a horse can mean head or back injuries. One lawsuit for negligence can end an otherwise prosperous business.

Stress safety with all instructors. Let students know you won't tolerate any "horseplay." Create a safety code and require strict adherence to its rules. Here are a few suggestions:

- Always require ASTM/SEI–labeled riding helmets for everyone who rides at your farm, whether student or boarder. (This goes for instructors as well). These helmets may not always be the most attractive, but they have been tested to be the safest. Make sure the hat and harness fit properly.
- Always require a boot or a sturdy shoe with a heel.
- Fit the horse and the tack to the rider. A small child needs a saddle and stirrups that are appropriate to prevent potential disasters.
- Keep all school tack clean, oiled, and in good repair. Dirty tack, such as stirrup leathers, can dry out and is more likely to break with pressure.
- Make sure your beginner horses are unflappable. Don't risk using a green horse when giving lessons. Constantly strive to improve and upgrade the quality of school horses in your string.
- Conduct safety drills with students and instructors. One drill requires each student to ride up to the instructor, recite a safety rule, and ride back to the team.
- It may be necessary to post signs in your barn, such as "Don't feed or pet the horses; they might bite," or "No smoking." Speed limit and "Horse Crossing" signs are also helpful.
- Require riders going on trail rides to travel in groups of at least two and, when possible, advise them to carry a cellular phone in a fanny pack.
- Enforce a policy of no alcoholic beverages allowed on the premises. Drinking alcohol and horse handling is a dangerous combination.
- If you have much activity in and out of your barn, you may want to make the traffic "one way" — have one entrance just for incoming traffic and the other for outgoing traffic.

INTERNATIONAL RIDING PROGRAMS

You may have seen advertisements for "Fox Hunting in Ireland," "Trail Rides in Wales," or "Pony Trekking in Lesotho, Africa."

Offering people from other countries the opportunity to see America from horseback can be big business. If you have the accommodations, an inviting setting, and a heart for internationals, this could be a profitable venture. International horse publications would be the best place to promote your program. For more information, contact J.A. Allen and Co., a noted British equestrian publisher, which has a store in London. (See Appendix M, page 148.)

BOARDING

My father owns a small apartment complex. He gets calls in the middle of the night from people complaining that neighbors are having a party, the faucet is dripping, or someone is illegally parked in their parking space. Having the title "landlord" in an apartment complex can be a thankless job. In contrast, walking into a barn in the morning and hearing whinnies and neighs from your stable of horses before the breakfast feeding is quite nice. These tenants will never call you "landlord."

Boarding other people's horses can be fun and advantageous or frustrating and unprofitable. First, figure out what level of boarding you want to provide. Some farms rent out the facility, but leave almost all other care, including feeding, up to a cooperative of boarders. They will charge less than a farm that provides all labor and management.

To ensure that boarding will be a profitable endeavor, conduct a price sensitivity analysis: Figure out what it will cost you, then what you need to charge to earn a profit. You'll want to be competitive with other farms in the area, so check to see what they charge. However, keep in mind that knowing what competitors charge does not tell you their costs. Their farms might not have a mortgage, or maybe they are not making a profit.

Once you've determined what set of prices can lead to a profit, the next step is to attract the clients. When determining a monthly charge, consider the type of clientele you want to attract; a barn specializing in training highly competitive hunters and jumpers or dressage horses will be able to charge considerably more than a barn that appeals primarily to trail riders. However, be prepared to offer a higher quality service for the higher price. For example, for the hunters and jumpers, you may have to put bell boots on when turning horses out, add feed supplements during periods of heavy

Remember the old saying, "The customer is always right." Be polite, and don't argue with clients.

training, and put blankets on and take them off during winter months. First apply the principles explained in Chapter 2 on advertising and promoting your business. To keep the clients you have once your boarding business is under way, you'll need to do the following:

- Make sure your barn is always clean and orderly. Boarders get upset when they pay you to clean stalls, only to find their beloved horses standing in dirty stalls with inadequate bedding. Muck out stalls *daily* and keep bedding clean and comfortable. Strip stalls as often as is needed to keep them clean, but as seldom as needed to save on bedding and labor costs. The frequency of stripping will vary with such factors as the individual horse and the type of flooring.

- Make sure horses have fresh, clean water available at all times. I once lost a boarder because her horse never had water in his bucket when she came to visit him. Samson, the horse, was watered daily at the same times as all the rest of the horses, and then two times in addition. As Samson drank he would take a few sips, then flip his bucket, spilling the water. I told my staff to be on special alert regarding his water supply, but the owner was concerned that her horse was being neglected and left the stable.

  In retrospect, I realized there was a solution. The horse could have been watered from a bucket that could be removed for cleaning, but otherwise was wedged into a corner-mounted feed pan that the horse couldn't budge.

Clients are more likely to view your business as well-run if the barn is orderly and well-kept.

© June Campbell

- If you also give riding lessons, balance the needs of boarders with students using school horses. Students may resent it if they are distracted from lessons by boarders exercising their horses, and boarders become frustrated if they have nowhere else to ride except an indoor arena where lessons are taking place. Prevent the two groups from getting in each other's way: when the weather is bad, post the student lesson schedule so boarders can plan to ride when the ring is relatively uncrowded.

  You might set aside a few hours a week in winter when the indoor arena is "for boarders only," to make them feel you are looking out for their riding needs as well.

- Demonstrate that you are a professional. Display in your office any diplomas, certificates, or trophies that you have, which will give students confidence in your abilities.

- Always show genuine concern for every horse in your care. Never disparage boarders or their horses. Even if they are criticizing their own horse, don't join in; it can come back to haunt you.

Require payment for boarding in advance. If this is not possible, don't let anyone get too far behind. Put a clause in the boarder's contract stipulating that you have the right to sell his horse to pay back board, but try to work it out; you could use the horse in lessons or lease the horse, or have the owner work for you to pay off back board. Be compassionate, but also practical.

LEASING

Leasing takes place when a horse is conveyed to someone for a specified term and rent. An exclusive lease provides that the lessee is the only rider permitted to ride the horse. (See the Equine Lease Agreement in Appendix C, page 127.) These leases work well for advanced students who are allowed to lease green horses or horses for sale, enabling you to earn money while getting your horse schooled and shown; beginning riders who are not yet ready to own and need a less advanced horse; or students who are "between" horses. Leasing often provides riders an opportunity to ride a higher quality or more experienced horse than they could afford to buy.

Instead of being exclusively leased, a good school horse can be more profitable if it is partially leased. A partial lease means that the lessee has use of the horse for a certain period of time, such as

Strive to accommodate the riding styles of your boarders. If there are both pleasure and horse show riders at your barn, don't conduct just horse shows. Organize some fun trail rides or other low-key events as well.

Wednesdays from 9 to 11 am, or on Mondays, Wednesdays, and Saturdays, for example. This enables you to continue using the horse in your lesson program while also receiving lease payments.

In a horse-sharing program there should be restrictions on how many hours per day each horse can be used to prevent the most popular horses from being overworked.

Partial Leasing = Profits

Multiple partial leases can be quite lucrative. For example, if you have eight riders who want to lease certain horses for one-hour sessions on certain days:

Rider A rides seven days a week @ $10/ride =	$300/month
Rider B rides three days a week @ $15/ride =	$180/month
Rider C rides three days a week @ $15/ride =	$180/month
Rider D rides three days a week @ $15/ride =	$180/month
Rider E rides twice a week @ $20/ride =	$160/month
Rider F rides once a week @ $25/ride =	$100/month
Rider G rides once a week @ $25/ride =	$100/month
Rider H rides once a week @ $25/ride =	$100/month
Monthly income from multiple partial leases =	$1,300

Lease-to-own is an agreement that enables a rider to purchase a horse over time. First a selling price is established and then the horse is leased for a certain period of time. When the time period has expired, the lessee may apply the lease amount paid to the purchase price of the horse. However, the lessee is under no obligation to purchase the horse.

Another variation on leasing is a horse sharing program. Riders pay a flat fee per month for access to all horses in the program. They can ride any horse in the program they choose, as long as no one else has signed up first to use the horse at the same time.

EXTRA SERVICES RENDERED

Many horse operations are struggling to make a profit without realizing the business opportunities available from offering additional services to their students and boarders. Consider the following financial opportunities for your operation.

Moneymaking Extras
- Grooming — brushing, bathing, mane pulling, braiding, trimming (muzzle and ears), body clipping
- Cleaning — tack, blankets, bandages, trailers
- Training — exercising, longing, halter-breaking, saddle-breaking, showing, driving, hunting, jumping, trailer loading

- Sales — leasing, multiple partial leasing, buying, selling, trading
- Boarding — full board (include grooming and exercising), regular board (stabling, feeding, and watering), pasture board (boarded in pasture and fed grass and hay only), additional turnouts, lay-ups (boarding and treating injured horses), geriatric board (taking care of retirees), brood mare board (special mare care and foaling check), stallion board (breeding)
- Judging (get your American Horse Show Association judge's card)
- Teaching — clinics, seminars, short courses, demonstrations
- Transportation — hauling horses and students to and from horse shows, and/or pickup and drop-off service for students taking lessons
- Catching and holding fee — when the veterinarian or farrier arrives
- Consulting — barn management, horse show management, farm and horse purchasing, agriculture, course designing
- Medications — first-aid treatment (ointments and sprays) and wrapping legs, "Bute," colic treatments, wormings. Lock the supply cabinet and make sure to charge for the use of these products. Some stables charge a yearly fee of about $75 to each boarder, which automatically covers any nonprescription medications provided and administered to horses. Others charge each time they administer medications to a horse.

6

Riding Camps

It takes a lot of work to conduct a summer horsemanship day camp or to have short camps during Christmas or spring break. These camps can be great fun, though, and be big money earners. You could also organize special-interest camps or clinics, such as a dressage or a roping camp. Themes in addition to horsemanship can be implemented, such as an equitation/etiquette camp, or an equestrian/computer camp.

This chapter focuses on summer riding camps for children. The fees you charge will depend on the going rates in your area, which generally vary from $150 to $350 per week for each student. If you teach 20 students a week for 12 weeks per summer at $250 per student, the gross earnings will be $60,000.

KEEPING COSTS DOWN

The two major costs associated with camps are the horses and the staff salaries. To reduce the cost of the horses, use as many boarder horses or borrowed horses as possible. Cut staff costs by allowing the counselors/instructors to ride school horses free of charge each week or take riding lessons in exchange for some of their work hours. If you are able to reduce these costs, you can expect to net a healthy profit margin.

ORGANIZING SESSIONS

Determine the length of camp sessions and daily hours. You could run one-week or two-week sessions during the months that schools are closed; two-week sessions require half the paperwork. A good length for a camp day is from 9 am to 4 pm. This allows enough time for campers to ride both in the morning and in the afternoon — since this is a horsemanship camp, parents will expect their children to ride as much as possible.

Although day-camp activities might officially cease at 4 pm, some parents may not be able to pick up their children until later, after they get off work. For these children, plan a relaxed, nonequestrian program and charge an additional fee, or have them work on the farm mucking out stalls, sweeping, or cleaning tack, to keep them busy and learning.

If you have a substantial number of campers, carefully consider how you organize their riding time. You could have all the students riding at the same time, which is horse- and ring-intensive, or you can break the campers into groups and have lectures and demonstrations for one group while the other group rides. The latter method reduces the number of horses you'll need and consequently the cost of operating the camp, but it also requires planning for the lectures.

If you have both very young campers and teenagers, organize activities for each age group separately, since their interests and abilities differ.

LUNCH SERVICE

Decide whether you want to require all campers to bring their own lunches and beverages daily, or if you want to give parents the option of paying you for providing meals. Parents with hectic work schedules might be willing and indeed eager to have you provide a boxed lunch for their children: a simple but nutritious sandwich, fruit, and a fruit drink. It may be too much work for your staff to take on this responsibility, but you might be able to have a catering service or local deli provide lunches. Add a nominal fee for your time spent setting up the lunches.

PRE-CAMP PLANNING TIPS

Successful Camp Organization

- Five months before your first session, send brochures about summer camp to all regular students and horse show and clinic participants. Begin running monthly ads in the local newspaper. (See Chapter 2 on advertising and promotion.)
- About the same time, put up posters at nearby elementary, junior, and senior high schools. Send an application for the camp to those who respond to your advertisements. (See sample Camp Form in Appendix E, page 129.)
- Two months before camp begins, plan the camp schedule, devise a curriculum (see below), and arrange for the counselors and a director. The ratio of counselors to campers

Use posters to advertise summer camp. Post them at local schools to generate student interest.

Summer Riding Camp at

Ten Oaks Riding Center

Two-week sessions beginning June 15
For Ages 8 to 16

- Basic Riding Skills
- Safe Horsemanship
- Trail Rides
- Games, Field Trips, and More!

It's fun! Sign up now!

For more information
call 555-555-5555
or pick up an application at
111 Center Blvd.
Centerville, MD 12345

☾ *Staff meetings should be held weekly so that problems can be addressed, which keeps up morale and improves the quality of your camp.*

depends on the riding levels of the students. Beginners generally require one counselor for every two to three campers; advanced riders can have one counselor for every six to eight campers. Fewer counselors means reduced labor costs; however, don't sacrifice safety and your reputation by hiring fewer counselors than needed.

- Appoint a director to be in charge of delegating responsibilities to the various counselors. These duties include scheduling activities, assigning horses, receiving payments, making sure liability release forms are signed before each rider starts camp, and anticipating and solving small problems that arise.

- The week before camp starts, conduct a training session for counselors and your director. The schedule, objectives, safety rules, and individual responsibilities should be discussed thoroughly. It is best to have a separate staff perform the barn work — feeding, watering, and mucking — and have the counselors handle the camp. However, if labor is in short supply, you can have the counselors do the barn work before and after camp, or you could develop a "barn management camp" for advanced students, putting them in charge of much of the work.
- Compile a task chart to make sure all jobs are assigned, such as filling the drink machine, making sure the water jug is filled, and watching every single camper until each is picked up by parents. Have counselors rotate tasks each week. This way, the work is shared equally and no one gets bored with the same chore all summer. It also provides a way for staff members to gain experience handling a variety of duties.

CAMP SAFETY

For the sake of your campers' well-being, their parents' peace of mind, and the horses, you must stress from the beginning that safety is a priority at your camp. Campers need to know there are boundaries. Print out, distribute, and post in several places camp safety rules that are strictly enforced. Have instructors review them frequently. These rules might include:
- No running or yelling around the horses.
- No eating, drinking, or chewing gum while riding.
- No jewelry is to be worn.
- Boots and helmet must be worn whenever mounted.
- Horses are *never* to be left in stalls with bridles on, and unless an instructor needs them for the next lesson, should not be left in stalls with their saddles on.
- Campers must lock stall doors after putting away their horses.
- A counselor must be notified immediately of any injury to horse, rider, or equipment.
- Always notify counselors of an early arrival or late departure.
- No camper is to leave the immediate premises, ever, unless on a supervised outing.

An additional word about injuries and accidents: If one occurs on your farm, write it down in a special notebook. Record exactly what happened, what first aid, if any, was rendered, and note if parents were contacted. This could be important information to have on hand if you are ever sued.

CAMP CURRICULUM

Develop a curriculum for each level of camper, and at the end of each camp session, award certificates of merit to each camper for mastering the lessons. The basic curriculum levels could be beginner, intermediate, and advanced; you could even devise one for the grand prix level if you wish. Examples of curricula for the first three levels appear below. You can change them or combine them up as you deem appropriate for your campers and teaching plans.

Beginner-Level Curriculum Goals

Campers will learn:
- The parts of the saddle
- The parts of the bridle
- Five major parts of the horse
- Three riding aids
- Basic grooming equipment used on a horse
- The five basic coat colors
- How to tell when a horse is adequately "cooled out"

Beginning campers should learn and be able to demonstrate basic grooming techniques.

Campers will be able to demonstrate:
- The proper way to approach a stabled horse
- How to groom and tack up, including picking up and cleaning hooves
- The correct way to lead a horse
- Mounting and dismounting techniques
- Walking, posting trot, and halting
- Riding a figure 8
- Mucking out a stall
- Haltering and unhaltering
- How to properly turn out a horse

Intermediate-Level Curriculum Goals

Campers will learn:
- The basic differences between good and poor conformation
- Basic horse rations
- Inoculations that horses must have annually
- How to take a horse's temperature
- The difference between a stallion, gelding, mare, colt, filly, and foal
- Two major parasites affecting horses and how to prevent them
- The step sequence for the walk, trot, canter, and gallop
- Cross-cantering and counter-cantering
- The aids used to ask a horse for the right and left leads

Campers will be able to demonstrate:
- Bathing a horse
- Pulling a mane
- How to disassemble, clean, and reassemble a saddle and bridle
- First aid for minor horse cuts
- Taking a horse's temperature
- How to braid a mane
- How to give and accept a leg up
- How to jump a two-foot course of fences
- Riding a figure 8 and a serpentine
- Posting on the correct diagonal and cantering on the correct lead
- Riding safely on the trail
- Posting to the trot without stirrups
- Blanketing and unblanketing a horse

Intermediate-level campers should be able to demonstrate specific riding skills.

Ross Chapple

Have campers identify the parts of English and Western saddles. I have included the answers above each box so you can copy the art to use in your own camp program.

The parts of an English saddle:
A. Pommel
B. Waist
C. Seat
D. Cantle
E. Skirt
F. Flap
G. Stirrup Iron
H. Stirrup Leather

Advanced-Level Curriculum Goals

Campers will learn:
- Ten parts of the horse's musculoskeletal system
- About floating teeth
- The gestation period of a mare
- How many teeth male and female horses have
- The age at which a junior rider loses junior status
- How many hands high is a small, medium, and large pony
- Four color breeds
- The official birthday of Thoroughbreds
- To identify a splint, a wind puff, and a bowed tendon
- The initial treatment for colic
- The amount of water horses require daily

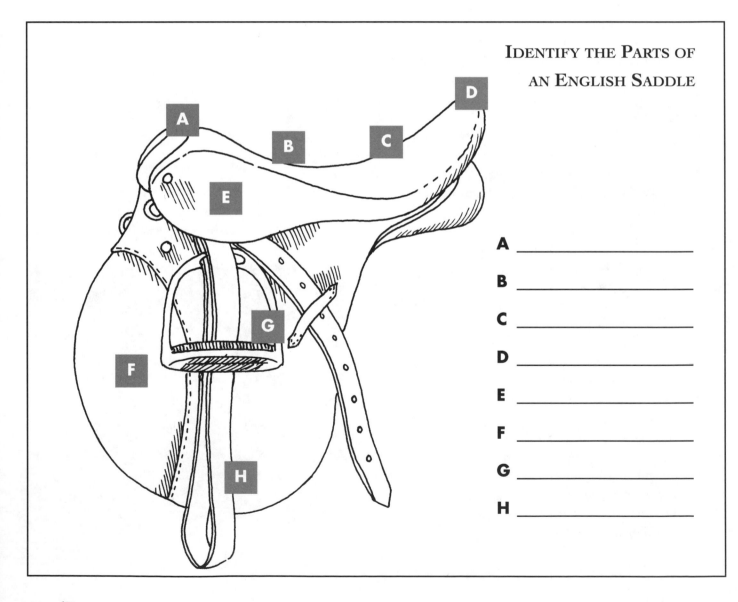

IDENTIFY THE PARTS OF AN ENGLISH SADDLE

A _____

B _____

C _____

D _____

E _____

F _____

G _____

H _____

Campers will be able to demonstrate:

- Braiding a tail
- Fitting a bridle and saddle
- Treatment for thrush
- Treatment for abscesses
- Longeing a horse
- How to prepare a bran mash
- Riding a three-foot course of fences
- Riding a cross-country course with two-foot jumps
- Simple and flying lead changes
- Turning on the forehand
- Jumping without stirrups

The parts of a Western saddle:

A. Horn
B. Pommel
C. Fork
D. Seat
E. Cantle
F. Latigo
G. Cinch Ring
H. Girth
I. Fender
J. Stirrup Leather
K. Stirrup
L. Flank Billet
M. Skirt

IDENTIFY THE PARTS OF A WESTERN SADDLE

A _____

B _____

C _____

D _____

E _____

F _____

G _____

H _____

I _____

J _____

K _____

L _____

M _____

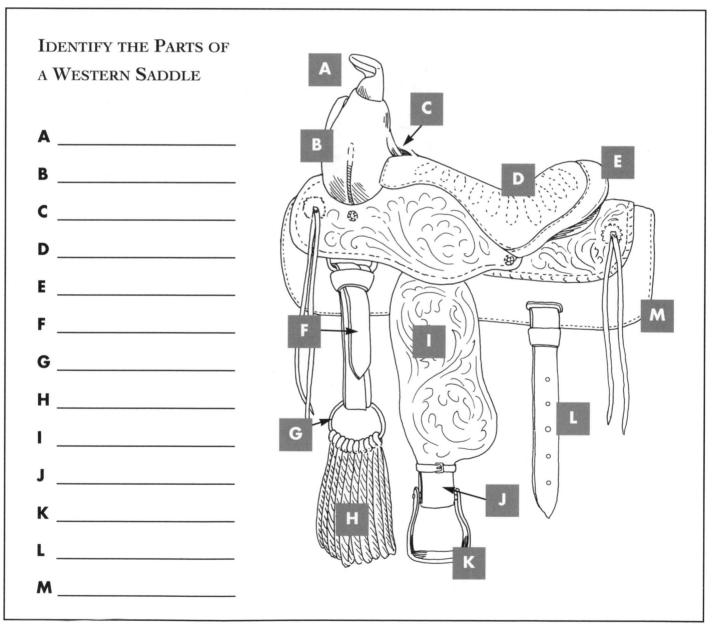

IDENTIFY THE PARTS OF THE HORSE

A _____   H _____   O _____

B _____   I _____   P _____

C _____   J _____   Q _____

D _____   K _____   R _____

E _____   L _____   S _____

F _____   M _____

G _____   N _____

A–crest, B–poll, C–forehead, D–muzzle, E–throatlatch, F–shoulder, G–knee, H–hoof, I–pastern, J–fetlock, K–cannon bone, L–chestnut, M–Coronary, N–hock, O–stifle, P–flank, Q–dock, R–back, S–withers

TYPICAL CAMP DAY

Each hour of every camp day should be planned ahead of time. The last thing you want is a group of campers standing around wondering what to do and later telling their parents they were bored. Specific activities should vary from day to day. Make sure the basic daily schedule is flexible, too, to accommodate special activities such as field trips. An example of a typical camp day follows.

9 am: Review events of the day and explain or reiterate safety rules. Students get a short lesson based on the curriculum for their level. Students groom and tack up, with assistance from instructors as necessary.

10:15 am: Mounted hour-long lesson, starting with mounted stretching exercises.

11:15 am: Students cool down horses, sponge if necessary, groom and put away tack.

Noon: Lunch break/games

1 pm: Listen to a ground lecture and watch a demonstration on subjects such as grooming for show or horse health. Consider asking your farrier or veterinarian to come one day and give a guest lecture during this time.

2 pm: Students groom again and tack up.

2:30 pm: Trail ride or mounted games and activities (see ideas below).

3:30 pm: Students cool down horses, groom, put away tack, and gather their belongings to leave at 4 pm.

Games and Activities

You'll want to have two lengthy lists of games and activities. One will be for activities on the ground and another list is for those played while mounted.

Campers can be divided into teams for some games and at the end of a camp session, each participant on the team with the most points receives a prize, such as a gift certificate for a few dollars to the tack shop or a small meal at the local fast-food restaurant. There should be no losers, of course, so give members of the other teams a prize, too. A description of some games follows; select the ones that are appropriate for the age and ability of your campers.

Ground Games

Balloon Pop. Everyone gets a balloon; the first one to blow it up, sit on it, and pop it wins! A variation can be played with water balloons — a refreshing treat for campers on a very hot day. To play, two lines are formed, about one yard apart. Players directly opposite each other are partners. The players in one line toss their balloons to their partners in the other line, and everyone takes one

Despite your best efforts to teach campers how to handle horses and about the basic rules of safety, there is a lot to learn and they will need to be reminded again and again.

Advanced students can compete over a cross-country course.

step back after each toss. Continue until there is only one set of children left with unbroken balloons. These are the winners. The same game can be played with eggs.

Horse Sense. Players are blindfolded, then try to identify certain parts of a very docile, live horse.

Carrot Bobbing. A carrot on a string is tied to each camper's waist and is left dangling about one foot from the seat of their britches. Each camper has to squat and try to get the carrot into a small coffee can on the ground. Campers can then feed the carrots to the horses.

Scavenger Hunt. Camp teams are each given a list of items they must find around the farm. The items might include a four-leaf clover, an oat kernel, a horse shoe, and a bell boot. The first team to come back with all the items wins.

Tack Test. Each player or team is given a bridle. At a signal, they take it completely apart. The first one to put it back together correctly wins.

Field Trip. Ride in the morning, then spend the afternoon taking campers to visit another type of horse operation. You could visit a farm with a completely different purpose from yours, your local equine rescue league, or an equine veterinary hospital. Arrange ahead of time for someone at the destination to give your campers a tour. First, however, make sure your insurance would cover you if any mishaps occur while transporting campers.

Horse Bowl. Players are divided into two groups. Various equine-related questions are asked. The team that answers the most questions correctly wins. Consider the age and level of ability of your campers when creating the questions. The questions can be presented in written form, or asked by an instructor much the way quiz games are set up. If the first team misses the question, the other team gets a chance to answer. Whichever team answers the most questions correctly is the winner.

Mounted Games

Flour and Dime Race. Riders from each team race up to a pie pan filled with flour. They leap off their ponies and blow the flour out of the pan until they reach a dime at the bottom. They hop back onto their mounts, and race to the finish line. The first team whose players all finish is the winner.

Egg Race. Team riders carry a raw egg on a spoon the length of the riding ring, one at a time at a walk. The team that gets the most whole eggs to the other side wins. For older children, you might require them to trot. This game also can be played with potatoes.

Horse Costume Day. Campers are advised to bring from home items that can be used to dress up their favorite horse. After a parade, counselors or the campers can vote to select the best costume. Take pictures to send home with the camper at the end of the session.

Equestrian Event Day. Campers organize and perform their own equestrian event.

Mock Fox Hunt. (See Chapter 7 for complete details.)

Dressage Mini-Show and Tea Party. Map out a dressage test ahead of time. Start off the event with a short lecture about the history of dressage. Campers then mount their horses, and each performs the same, small portion of the dressage test as you talk him through. Have counselors judge the contestants. Give the winner a blue ribbon, and award red ribbons to all other participants. Follow with a bona fide tea party. (See Chapter 7 for a menu.)

PARENTS DAY

One of the best ways to show parents what they got for their money is to ask them to be present the afternoon of their child's last day at camp. This is when the children can show their family and friends all that they have learned and how much fun camp has been.

Plan the show carefully. Start out with the more formal events, when you will want campers to look neat and tidy. Then move on to the more boisterous activities. The events of the afternoon might go in this order:

- Campers groom horses appropriately for show, braiding manes, polishing hooves, and so on, just before parents arrive.

Warn your counselors and instructors to be alert — and patient — at all times.

☺ Serve snacks and refreshments to parents while campers untack, groom, and put horses in stalls.

- Walk/trot class
- Command class
- Favorite mounted game, such as the flour and dime or the egg race
- Horse Costume Parade
- Award team prizes

Chances are that parents will sign up their children for camp next year. If your camp proves to be a financial success and you have the facilities, consider offering an overnight camp and earn an even greater profit. Don't forget to do a partial budget as explained in Chapter 4 to ensure that an overnight camp will be profitable.

Offer a certificate of merit for campers' achievements. Another sample certificate appears in Appendix F.

TEN OAKS RIDING CENTER

111 Center Blvd.
Centerville, MD 12345
555-555-5555

This is to certify that _____ has successfully completed the Ten Oaks Riding Center Program. The undersigned have here unto affixed their signatures and the crest of Ten Oaks Riding Center this_____ day of_____, _____.

_____   _____
Owner   Manager

7
Moneymaking Events and Ideas

Many horse operations already conduct moneymaking programs, such as camps, which are major endeavors. They could increase profits by supplementing those programs with short-term events that bring in money, promote the business, but require less planning and personnel. This chapter is chock full of ideas to help you toward this end.

HORSE SHOWS

You may think that putting on a horse show is beyond your abilities. Provided you have the facilities and the personnel, though, running such an event can be a profitable and an enjoyable undertaking.

First, consider the participants for the show. What is your target audience? Do you have many beginners, intermediate students, or even advanced students? What are their needs? Will you conduct a schooling show or a rated show? If, for example, you have a large number of green horses that need mileage, then you should have a schooling horse show. Whatever show you decide on, remember to keep the atmosphere relaxed and fun.

Schooling/Open Shows
Schooling/open shows are good confidence-builders for riders and horses and often spur them on to better performances. They also expose parents and grandparents to the horse world. Often, proud parents, seeing their children show a horse, will sign them up for additional lessons. They may even lease or purchase a horse.
Show Class Ideas
- **School horses only.** This class is open to all horses used by riding schools for teaching lessons.
- **Lead-line.** Students must be under six years old.
- **Golden oldies.** Entrants must be over 45 years old.
- **Baby or pre-green.** These are schooling classes for horses in their first six months of showing.

If you make the schooling shows open to riders from other farms, you never know — some of them just might decide to stay.

- **Dollar bill.** Each rider holds a dollar bill under one knee at the walk, trot, and canter. Whoever keeps it there the longest wins. No chaps or shorts allowed!
- **Pairs.** Two riders are judged at the walk, trot, and canter as they ride almost knee-to-knee.
- **Costume.** Riders dress themselves and their horses in costumes of their choice or according to a theme. They are judged on creativity and originality.
- **Local hunter.** This class is open to horses stabled within 50 miles of the show grounds.
- **Short stirrup.** Only riders under the age of 10 are eligible to participate.
- **Jack Russell terrier races.** This is a great spectator event to run when the judge is taking a lunch break. Construct a starting box for about six dogs or have the owners hold the dogs until the race is signaled to begin. A fox tail on a rope attached to a reel can be pulled down the course for the dogs to chase. The finish line consists of bales of hay stacked to allow a single dog in at a time. Add small jumps to make the course more exciting.

   Tag the dogs with different colors to make identification easier for the judges. If you have enough entries, the class can be divided into heats; the two winning dogs in each heat compete for the grand prize.

   At the Washington International Horse Show, the races are videotaped and played back in slow motion on the big overhead screen. You can videotape races at your shows as well, and play them back on video nights. I guarantee, they'll provide some hilarious entertainment.

RATED SHOWS

If you determine that you have a more advanced target audience consisting of students and horses that are more competitive and need points, you can have a rated show. Contact the American Horse Show Association for further information (see Appendix L, page 146, for the address).

Horse Show Associations

If the level of your target audience is somewhere between a schooling show and a rated show, you may want to join or form a local association that organizes several horse shows every year. Points that are won at each show are added up at year's end, and the leaders are the champions of your horse show association. You could also sponsor a year-end awards banquet to honor winners and raise money for a local veterinary school or equine rescue league.

Show Planning Calendar

Managing a horse show takes a lot of organization and delegation. For your first show especially, it's worth the money to get quality jumps, ribbons, trophies, and a good judge. Your extra effort will give you a good reputation and bring more participants to future shows.

Six to 12 months before the show:

Book the judge, decide on the classes, and print the program flyer, including the prize list. (Include a horse show checklist; it can be sent as a gift with the prize list. See the example below.) Ask one or two local vendors, including tack and feed stores, to advertise in the flyer to offset the cost of promoting the show. The cover of the prize list should include the location, date, time, judge, and a rain date of the show.

The inside of the prize list should include the list of classes, entry fees for each class, and rules, including prizes to be awarded.

Your rules might say that all horses must come with evidence of a current negative Coggins test, dogs must be leashed at all times, riders must wear hard hats while mounted, and the farm and its employees are not responsible for any accident, injury, or loss occurring during the show. It might also explain that a trophy and six ribbons will be awarded in all classes, and a Championship trophy and ribbon and Reserve Championship ribbon will be awarded in the following divisions (then list according to classes planned).

Three to six months in advance, you'll need to:

- Order the ribbons, exhibitors' numbers, and judge's cards.
- Secure the announcer, judge, show secretary, course designer, jump crew, runners, and gateman (call to confirm two weeks before the show).
- Organize a concession stand and arrange for personnel.
- Obtain a public address system or megaphones.

One month in advance:

- Rent several portable toilets, if necessary. Buy sufficient toilet paper.
- Secure adequate trash receptacles and arrange for emptying.
- Have equipment, such as jumps, painted as needed.
- Ask local emergency medical personnel to be on hand for the show.

The day before the show:

- Disk and drag rings.
- Get change for the cash box.
- Mow grass.
- Set up the first course.
- Put up signs and directional arrows since riders and the judge will start showing up at 7 am.
- Clearly mark parking area, water faucets, entry booth, and so on.
- Organize ribbons and trophies for each class.

Entry fees should be competitive with comparable shows in the area; otherwise, riders just might forgo your show to ride in the less costly ones.

On the day of the show:
Keep the show moving along. Recheck all points before awarding championships. Provide the judge with food and drink.
- Post course designs for classes.
- Provide clipboard, judge's cards, and pencils for judge.
- Make sure jump crew knows when to change fences and to what height.
- Be sure to check each horse for negative Coggins test.
- Post judge's cards.
- Pay the judge, announcer, and other assistants.
- Pray for good weather and a good turn out (but remember, you planned a rain date).

The day after the show:
- Make sure all trash is collected.
- Return all rented equipment, before it gets broken.

HORSE SHOW CHECKLIST

Horse Supplies
- ✓ Coggins test results
- ✓ Membership card
- ✓ Saddle
- ✓ Pad
- ✓ Girth
- ✓ Bridle
- ✓ Martingale
- ✓ Halter
- ✓ Extra bits
- ✓ Splint boots
- ✓ Bellboots
- ✓ Leadline
- ✓ Crop
- ✓ Hay and hay net
- ✓ Buckets
- ✓ Extra reins
- ✓ Body brush

- ✓ Dandy brush
- ✓ Finishing brush
- ✓ Hoof pick
- ✓ Mane comb
- ✓ Sweat scraper
- ✓ Curry comb
- ✓ Fly spray
- ✓ Braiding kit
- ✓ Rubber bands
- ✓ Yarn
- ✓ Scissors
- ✓ Coat polish
- ✓ Hoof dressing
- ✓ Shampoo
- ✓ Baby powder
- ✓ Vaseline
- ✓ Baby wipes
- ✓ First aid kit

Rider Supplies
- ✓ Hat
- ✓ Coat
- ✓ Ratcatcher and collar
- ✓ Pants, boots, socks, or knee-highs
- ✓ Collar pin or monogrammed collar
- ✓ Gloves
- ✓ Raincoat and hat cover
- ✓ Spurs
- ✓ Jumping vest
- ✓ Hairnet
- ✓ Rubber boot covers
- ✓ Safety pins, needle, and thread
- ✓ Pain reliever
- ✓ Visor or baseball cap
- ✓ Sunscreen
- ✓ Sunglasses
- ✓ Hand towels
- ✓ First aid kit

© Genie Stewart-Spears

EDUCATIONAL ACTIVITIES

Offer events such as short courses, seminars, and clinics to advertise your business, generate revenue, and educate you and your students. Try to bring in a well-known, reputable judge or horse trainer; she'll add credibility to the event and draw more participants.

ENDURANCE OR COMPETITIVE TRAIL RIDES

Hosting an endurance or competitive trail ride can be a great way to get to know others in the area and stimulate interest in the sport. Trail rides vary in length, with a suggested range anywhere between 10 and 100 miles.

On a trail ride, the conditioning and endurance of horse and rider are put to the test. Competitors ride over a predetermined trail. Horses should be closely monitored throughout the ride for soundness and signs of exhaustion, and have their pulse and respiration taken at designated checkpoints. The first horse and rider to cross the finish line after successfully making it through the checkpoints wins.

In order to make this a profitable venture, your budget must include an entry fee sufficient to cover the cost of assistants,

Host an endurance ride to draw business, and charge an entry fee to cover your costs.

Shown above is Valerie Kanavy on two-time World Champion "Pieraz."

veterinarians, markers, flyers, mailings, and your time. For more information, contact your local trail ride association or veterinarian.

HUNTER PACES

Hunter Paces are a fun and profitable alternative to a horse show. Generally, they require less equipment and effort on your part than a full-fledged horse show or event. You can set courses for beginning to advanced students.

Brightly colored plastic ribbons mark the course. Participants look for the ribbons, much the way they would have to "listen" for the foxhounds, to know the right direction in which to ride. You can even play prerecorded "hound music" at certain points. There is more than one way to organize a Hunter Pace event. One way is to come up with a predetermined "optimal time." If you estimate the optimal (not necessarily the fastest) time to ride the course is 30 minutes, whichever rider comes in closest to that time wins. The rider who finishes in 29 minutes, wins, for instance, not the one who finishes in 28 minutes, because this is not a speed race. You could also award prizes for the fastest and the slowest times.

Award ribbons and trophies to the winners. Send press releases to your local papers before and after the event (see Chapter 2).

MOCK FOX HUNT

An event that all your students, boarders, and those from outside barns can enjoy is the Mock Fox Hunt. This is really just a glorified trail ride with treats and prizes for all participants. The organization of such an event is simple and, with a little imagination, should result in a fun-filled ride for everyone.

Fox Hunt Tips
- Charge a "capping fee," which is the amount of money that hunts usually charge guests who join them. You can charge participants, including your students, an additional fee for the use of your horses.
- Set a date and time.
- Go over the route in advance to eliminate any last-minute surprises.
- Organize your "hunt club" and select your "hunt colors." Matching sweatshirts or other clothing is a fun idea and will build camaraderie. You could ask each participant to buy a farm sweatshirt, or include the cost of the shirts in your capping fee.

♘ *Hunter Pace events can be promoted exclusively in your own barn or advertised to the general public.*

- It makes the day more interesting for the uninitiated if they have at least a small grasp of hunting terms. Below is a list that can be copied and given to the mock fox hunters.

Fox-Hunting Terminology

The *Master of Foxhounds*, or MFH, is the boss. The *Huntsman* controls the hounds, and the *Whippers-In* help the Huntsman. The *Hunt Secretary* collects the capping fee and dues, while the *field* is made up of all the mounted *followers*. The followers can be divided into a first and a second field. The more advanced riders, who make up the first field, jump the obstacles. The second field, which is slower, is composed of less experienced riders. They delicately avoid any object that may unsettle their horses or themselves. You might want to invite parents or friends to follow on foot as spectators.

The *brush* is the fox's tail. The *cry* is the sound the fox hounds make while hunting. If you hear someone say the fox *goes to ground*, it means he is hiding, usually underground. The *scent* is the smell of the fox that the hounds follow. *Ware* is an abbreviation for beware, as in "ware wire" or "ware hole."

Designate staff members as the Master of Foxhounds, Huntsman, Whippers-In, and Hunt Secretary. They can wear matching jackets or perhaps pin their titles to their backs to distinguish themselves from the rest of the field.

Design a fox outfit and appoint someone to wear the costume and then hide out at a designated place at the end of the course.

The course can be tracked by actually following the sightings of the "fox" or it can be marked out with riddles leading to the next area of chase. For example, "The fox's tail is colored red, find the next clue behind the shed!" You get the idea.

To add effect, pipe in "hound music" at the clue points. The "hunt" culminates when the fox is found. The fox can then hand out candy or other treats, and everyone returns to the barn.

After the hunt, all participants, including parents and guests who didn't ride, head to the house for Brunswick stew (see the recipe at right) or a big hunt breakfast. Prepare the meal ahead of time and charge guests a fee, or everyone can provide the ingredients.

This social event gives your barn great exposure and creates good public relations with the parents who pay the bills. It is also a noncompetitive event; the pleasure riders at your barn who do not participate in other horse events can join in this good time.

Dressage Show and Tea Party

Consider a dressage show for students and boarders. Open it up to those from other farms if you want, and invite parents,

---

BRUNSWICK STEW

This classic Virginia Hunt Country recipe traditionally is made with chicken and cooked over an open fire in a cast-iron pot. You could also cook it in a big pot on the stove.

2 5-pound hens
4 quarts water
7 medium-sized potatoes, diced
4 1-pound cans of lima beans
2 1-pound cans of corn
4 1-pound cans of tomatoes
4 large onions, chopped
1 cup tomato paste
Salt and pepper to taste

Note: Frozen or fresh vegetables can be substituted for canned ones.

1. Cook the chickens in the water for 1 hour. Remove from the cooking pot and debone. Cut up the meat and return to the pot.
2. Add the potatoes, lima beans, corn, tomatoes, onions, tomato paste, and salt and pepper to taste. Cook for 1 hour, stirring occasionally. (Take care not to scorch the bottom of the pot.)

15 to 20 servings

siblings, and grandparents to watch the show and attend the party. Riding contestants can be judged by your own qualified instructors or by guest judges.

Afterward, have an authentic British tea party. Charge enough per contestant and guest to cover your costs and make a profit.

Host a traditional tea party after a dressage show for students and boarders.

CONTESTS

Photo, video, literary, art, horse bowl, or horse judging contests are all great ways to stimulate interest in your barn.

Photo contests require entrants to submit photos they have taken themselves of their own horses, or of the stable horses. Contestants choose the captions. Post the winners on your bulletin board in full view for visitors to see.

VHS videos, 15 minutes in length or shorter, can be educational or amusing. Consider the best horse safety video, horses at play, before and after a year's worth of riding lessons, or how *not* to clean a stall.

Literary contestants submit either a poem or an essay (1,500 words or less) on a horse-related topic; it can be serious, such as the proper way to treat a colicky horse, or fun, such as why your horse is your best friend in 100 words or less.

Judge art contestants on their creativity and the overall appearance of their work. Display entries in the office.

Organize horse bowl competitions to test knowledge in horse-related topics. This is a fast-paced game of recall complete with buzzers. Four players on each team sound a buzzer and must correctly answer the questions before the other team does.

Horse judging contests consist of several classes of horses brought out and evaluated by contestants. A qualified instructor should make the official placing. After the contestants have judged the classes, they must defend their rationale for placing classes in a certain order. This is known as giving "oral reasons." Contestants who place the class correctly and give good oral reasons for their decisions are the winners.

Require a small entry fee for each contest. Distribute ribbons, trophies, tack, a free lesson, or cash awards to the winners. Make sure you charge enough to make a profit, covering both your expenses and your time.

RAFFLES

Have you ever had a horse you couldn't give away? Well, here's what to do. Organize a raffle — it's a great way to get your entire barn involved in moving the horse.

Once the neighbor's nondescript stallion (actually, I could describe him but let's be kind) broke through the fence and bred one of our school pony mares. We had no use for a pony colt and couldn't sell it for much, so we decided to put him up for raffle. My students sold tickets and the person with the most sales won a prize. We made over $600 and the winner was delighted to get a colt for a $2 ticket.

PUBLIC TRAIL RIDES

Offering trail rides can be a great financial opportunity. This is true particularly if it brings in long-term customers.

The first and last exposure to riding many people have is renting a trail horse by the hour. Be sure to make the experience as enjoyable as possible by providing clients with well-behaved horses. Have an experienced instructor or rider lead the ride at a pace appropriate for the group's level of experience. Give a quick lesson on how to get a horse to go and stop, even for those riders who say they have ridden horses before. On the trail, if a rider is having trouble with a horse, take the time to find out why, and if necessary, swap horses with the rider.

For longer trail rides, don't be afraid to be creative. A stable in Virginia offers romantic trail rides. They guide riders to a secluded

Note: Raffles are not legal everywhere. Be sure to check the laws in your state before conducting a raffle.

moonlit spot, provide a picnic, and let them wander back to the barn at their leisure. Others offer cowboy coffee and grub at the halfway point. You could have an Indian artifact excursion ride, chuck wagon with singing cowboys or singalongs, or a Civil War or Revolutionary War ride if you live in an area with historical sites.

Attract trail riders by offering discount rates to church groups, civic organizations, and schools.

After taking a group out on a trail ride, offer your farm brochure and event calendar to the riders. Let them know that you offer riding lessons.

HAYRIDES

Hayrides are another fun and profitable venture. Promote hayrides using the ideas in Chapter 2. If people have a good time and are interested in horses, perhaps they'll be interested in hearing about other events and services you offer.

As with trail rides, you can bring in more hayriders by offering discount rates to groups.

DRINK MACHINES

These may have little to do with horses directly, but providing soft drink machines is a service to visitors and will generate a small income for you. The drink companies supply the machines, deliver the drinks, and do all the maintenance and repairs.

Depending on your selling price and the profit margin in your area, you can earn $.15–$.30 on each can. If you sell 20 drinks every day and earn $.20 per drink, you will have increased your profits by over $1,400 at the end of the year.

♘ *Use the drink machine to add more fun to your school by requiring students who fall off to buy their instructor a soda!*

8
Buying and Selling Horses

As you continue through this book, you'll realize that there are many moneymaking opportunities available in the horse business. Buying and selling horses can be one of the more lucrative ones, but you must do your homework and devise a careful plan.

PRIVATE CONTRACT SALES

The process of buying and selling horses to and from individuals is known as private contract sales. No matter what kind of horse business you have, buying and selling horses can be a great financial opportunity.

Since there isn't any Blue Book on horses, an animal's value can vary from sale to sale. A horse that may be worth only $750 to you may be worth $2,500 to someone else. Don't be afraid to ask the highest, but still fair, price for your horses.

The secrets to making money on your purchases are:
- Buy low
- Turn over quickly
- Sell for top dollar
- Be a salesperson

Buy Low

To buy low, you have to have a good network. Develop a contact at the race track and the veterinarian's office. When they come across a buyer who wants to sell a horse quickly, have them call you. Once I was at the veterinarian's office when someone was trying to sell a horse to another customer. The mare didn't pass the veterinarian's examination because of a severe case of thrush. The owner was so frustrated that she sold me the horse for $500. After a few months of treatment, I sold the mare for $3,000 and made a healthy profit. Sometimes it just takes being in the right place at the right time and a willingness to take some risk.

Turn Over Quickly

Avoid investing too much time and expense on your purchase. To do this, predict how long it will take to get the horse in shape to be sold for a profit. If you have the opportunity to purchase or are given a very thin, malnourished horse, the initial price will be low, but by the time you pay for veterinary bills, shoes, feed, supplements, and training, the total amount of time and money invested in the horse may never be recovered.

Horse people can be eternal optimists, always thinking a particular horse will improve with just a few more training sessions and then it will sell for big bucks. Be realistic. Some horses are just problem horses and will take an eternity to straighten out. In this situation, it is better to bail out early rather than to invest endlessly. Remember the saying, "Let your profits run long and cut your losses short."

For example, Sue bought a 6-year-old Thoroughbred named Kala off the track without trying her out in the hopes of turning her into a show hunter. After a year of training, Kala had progressed very little. When Sue tried to sell the mare for $2,500, many people came to try out Kala, but only one made an offer of $500. Sue refused to sell at such a loss, so she invested another year's worth of board, veterinary bills, and farrier bills, totaling about $3,500. She would have been wiser to pocket the $500 and save $3,500 in bills.

Sell for Top Dollar

Strive to sell the horse at its peak conditioning, ability, and performance levels. Perception matters. A well-conditioned, well-groomed horse will sell better than a thin horse, even if the unattractive animal is actually a better horse overall.

⚘ A 45-minute clip and clean-up job can make or break the deal and potentially add hundreds of dollars to the sale price.

Be a Salesperson

Constantly network. Get involved with activities that put you in contact with potential customers. Judge shows, join local, state, or national horse associations, and participate in charity events. Host promotional events (see Chapter 2), and hand out your business cards and a list of horses you are currently selling.

Put up "For Sale" signs in tack and feed shops and at veterinary clinics. Include a color snapshot or photocopy of the horse. Post tear-off tabs of paper with your phone number and horse-for-sale at the bottom.

Before any potential buyers arrive, get organized. Have available all the information on the horses' selling points, such as show or race records, pedigree, pictures, or videos. If the clients

Margaret Thomas

Buying and selling horses can be a great financial opportunity, but avoid investing too much time and expense on your purchase.

are not in the area, mail this information to them. When they come, be hospitable.

Take action during the last part of a customer's visit. Promote the horse without being overbearing. This takes finesse and practice. Be honest and direct in stressing all of the horse's good points, but don't lie about its weaknesses if you are asked. Ask about the potential buyer's level of expertise, intended use, and likes and dislikes and then talk about the horse's strengths, experience, and personality in this context. For example, by asking questions you learn that the rider is an advanced beginner to intermediate rider, would like to have a horse to bring to local shows and enjoy on trail rides, and wants a fairly quiet, dependable horse. So, in talking about the horse for sale, you mention that he has been shown successfully for the past three years (mention specific shows and placings if you know them), has been ridden by some of your students who are just learning to jump and trail ridden by others, and has excellent manners in the stall and under tack.

Always say yes when negotiating. For example, "Yes, I would like to sell him for that price, but his potential in the show ring makes his value considerably higher," or "Yes, I'll sell him for that price if you trade me the pony you've outgrown." Hold a horse only if you get a deposit.

Finally, if the customers aren't interested in one horse, keep their names on file and contact them when you find another, more suitable horse for them. Keep them on your mailing list for shows, newsletters, tack sales, and promotional events.

Commissions

A commission is the fee you receive for performing a certain service. Your time, training, and experience are valuable, and shouldn't be given away. When purchasing or selling products for clients, add 10 to 15 percent to the sale price for your commission. This includes selling and buying horses.

When selling a horse for someone, be sure to get a written contract that specifies the selling price (the amount desired as well as the lowest acceptable amount), liability issues (who pays if the horse is sick, injured, or killed), the commission you will receive at the time of the sale, and the period of time you have in which to sell the horse.

There should be an exclusivity clause that guarantees your commission should any other party sell the horse during this time period. In two instances, I lost commissions. In the first instance, the buyer went around me and purchased the horse directly from my client, who subsequently never paid my commission. In the second instance, I was forced to purchase a horse I had on commission that was badly injured while in the process of being sold. Learn from my mistakes: be sure to spell out terms and get everything in writing.

Let tack shops, trailer suppliers, and other agents know when you refer business to them. Try to work in a commission or arrange for a discount on products you purchase from them.

HORSE AUCTIONS AND SALES

Selling your horses through auctions or horse sales can save you time in setting up appointments and showing horses to customers. You'll make even more money if you stage the auction or sale yourself.

Professional Auctions

To give you a better idea of how an auction works, I'll use information from a professional auction company as an example. This company advertises nationally and locally, and it publishes a brochure listing each horse it handles, which is sent to over 4,000 prospective buyers on a mailing list. It produces and mails to interested buyers a catalog that gives detailed information on each horse consigned in a sale.

Often, the seller gets these services for less than the cost of a few classified ads and pays less commission than an agent would charge. The company advises that you put up displays and decorate your stall to draw attention to your horse. To get a good price, your horse should be healthy, fit, carrying good weight, and be well groomed.

You can set a minimum price on your horse so you aren't forced to take a low bid. If you sell the horse in the ring above your minimum price, you will receive a check from the auction company shortly thereafter.

Before selling your horse this way, check out various auction companies with other horse owners in your area to make sure the one you select is reputable. Other horses owners can also educate you about the various buyers that frequent auctions, and tell you which ones run operations where horses are well cared for and which do not. With this information, and by using your right to refuse a low price, you can minimize the risk that your horse will end up in bad hands or be resold by the pound.

You can make a profit by selling your horses through auctions or horse sales.

If you are completely unfamiliar with horse auctions and sales, attend several before holding your own.

Holding an Auction at Your Farm

By holding an auction or sale yourself, you can avoid sales commissions and entry fees. Your profits will include commissions on horses you sell for others and entry fees.

Holding an auction or sale on your farm also is a great way to bring in new business. Those who come might end up as boarders and students.

An auction also is a way to liquidate your operation if ever the need arises. I once worked at a stable that lost its lease after many years, and the woman who managed the business could not sell the horses, equipment, or even the client list to the new operators moving in.

The manager decided to have a liquidation auction. She advertised and sent a sale catalog to every student, boarder, exhibitor, and guest who had visited the farm over the course of many years.

The horses were meticulously groomed, people turned out in droves, and the bidding was incredibly high. Everything sold, right down to the last pitchfork, for more than she expected. In many instances, current and former students bought the horses on which they had learned to ride.

To hold an auction at your farm, research local, state, and federal licensing laws or hire a professional auction company. Most states have stringent licensing laws for auctioneers and auction houses. If you hire a professional company, get recommendations from others in the horse business, and find a licensed and bonded company that has been in business for some time. A well-run company will have someone who consults carefully with you over planning and operation of the sale.

Promoting the Auction

Once you're confident about the inner workings of such an event, think about the audience you want to reach, and advertise in periodicals that reach that audience. (See list of periodicals in Appendix M, page 148.) And don't forget to advertise on the Internet.

Coordinate this advertising with a sequential mailing. The following section explains a five-piece mailing, based on one used by a professional auction company. It gives detailed examples to follow in promoting a horse sale or auction.

The mailing announces the sale, and enlists and informs consigners and buyers. It consists of a postcard, consignment forms, consignor's letter and information sheets, brochure, and a full catalog, respectively.

Sequence of Mailings:
1. Send a postcard to announce the date of sale, and so on.
2. Mail consignors the forms that were requested. Mail

these forms also to a regular list of consignors and anyone else who may be interested. You will need to have an attorney familiar with the horse industry provide you with a consignment form that protects you from liability. If you hire a professional auction company, it might provide this type of form. Be aware that liability laws differ from state to state.

3. Next, consignor's letters are sent to those who consign. See the consignor's information in Appendix I.

4. Send a brochure to your entire mailing list. Mail the brochure first class, which will help you update your mailing list. If people have moved and the brochure is returned, for instance, you can eliminate them from your list. Respond to any requests for more information generated by the brochure.

5. Finally, the last part of the five-piece mailing — the full catalog — is mailed. It is sent to sellers — those who requested a full catalog, and a short list of "regulars." Your catalog should be tailored to fit your specific situation.

The cover of the catalog should include sale name, date, location, features, and information contacts. The inside cover should have welcoming statements, schedule, and sale personnel, as well as important notices such as:

- Please read and familiarize yourself with conditions of the sale. (The conditions of the sale is something else you should obtain from the auction company or your attorney.)

- There is no implied warranty made by the auctioneer as to the merchantability or fitness for particular purpose of any animal offered for sale in this auction. All responsibility lies between the consignor and the buyer.

- Prospective bidders are cautioned that warranties on horses purchased are only as stated in the conditions of sale.

- Veterinary assistance is available at bidder's expense on request to auctioneer. Examine horses before bidding.

- Buyer has the right to have a veterinary examination within 12 hours of the start of the session in which the horse sells and before the horse leaves the sale grounds.

- Registration papers will be mailed to AQHA for transfer for Quarter horses and to the buyer for other breeds not earlier than 30 days after the sale for horses paid for by check.

- All sales made on the sale grounds must be through the office.

A catalog is part of a coordinated mailing program designed to promote your horse sale or auction.

Ten Oaks
Riding Center

Horse Auction
August 17, 1997
10 a.m. to 2 p.m.

111 Center Blvd.
Centerville, MD 00000

Contact **Connie Smith**
for more information.

555/555-555

- A paid receipt or release is required to remove any horse from the sale grounds.
- Visa and MasterCard are accepted with a 5% buyer's premium.
- All sales are subject to the state sales tax unless buyer has a valid Dealer's Registration and signs proper state tax form, or buyer signs state tax form that horse is purchased for breeding purposes only.

Catalogs often list personnel associated with the sale, including auctioneers, announcer, ring men, and sale veterinarian. In addition, the catalog should provide an index of consignors, and an alphabetical index of horses to be sold at auction. The conditions of the sale can be printed on the inside back cover.

☙ Remember to use the sale as a marketing tool for your farm's products and services.

Horse Sale Planning Calendar

Six to 12 months before the sale:
- Decide upon the type of sale and your target audience.
- Book the auction company, and ask for any suggestions on planning the sale. Schedule a rain date.
- Print your postcards, consignor's letters, and information sheets.
- Begin the five-piece mailing.

Three to six months in advance:
- Begin compiling catalog.
- Order the consignor's numbers.
- Secure the office staff, announcer, ring men, barn staff, sale veterinarian, runners, and gate man.
- Organize a concession stand and arrange for personnel.
- Obtain public address system or megaphones.

One month in advance:
- Mail catalog.
- Rent Port-a-Potties, if necessary. Buy sufficient toilet paper.
- Provide adequate trash receptacles and arrange for emptying.
- Paint equipment (such as jumps) as needed.
- Ask local rescue squad personnel to be on hand for the sale, if necessary.

Two weeks in advance:
- Call to confirm the auctioneers, announcer, ring men, concessionaires, office and barn staffs, sale veterinarian, gate men, and runners. Give them directions and arrival times.

The day before the sale:
- Disk and drag rings.
- Get change for the cash boxes, concessions, and tack shop.

- Mow grass.
- Set up jumps in practice ring.

Sale day:
- Check for negative Coggins tests.
- Put up signs and directional arrows.
- Clearly mark parking area, water faucets, sale office, and so forth.
- Make sure the jump crew knows when to change fences and to what height.
- Give auctioneers, ring men, and announcer food and drink throughout the day.
- Keep the sale moving along quickly.
- Pay all the hired personnel.
- Make sure all complaints are handled properly and all financial matters, including vet certificates and registration papers, are filed.
- Pray for good weather and a good turnout!

The day after the sale:
- Make sure all trash is collected.
- Return all rented equipment, before it gets broken.
- Put all the money you made in a high-earning cash investment!
- Figure out when the checks will clear, and prepare to handle registration transfers and other paperwork in the specified time period.
- Make a list of areas that need improvement for the next sale and follow through in making changes.

The information above should help you hold your own horse sale. Be sure the grounds are in excellent shape and really showcase your operation. If you have a tack shop, stock up on products that may be needed at a sale — shampoo, braiding equipment, fly spray. Enticing sales may bring an additional profit.

Have plenty of farm brochures with inserts stating services readily available. Camp brochures and horse show schedules also should be plentiful. Make sure the announcer promotes upcoming events at your farm as well as the tack shop and concession sales.

9
Breeding Horses

Establishing an active breeding program on your farm has good moneymaking potential, but be forewarned: It is far more complicated than simply getting two animals together for mating purposes, and without good planning you could lose a lot of money.

Many horse owners, in an effort to extend the usefulness of their mares, go into the breeding business. They figure they can sell the offspring profitably. However, unless you are ready to invest substantial capital and unless there is a strong market for yearlings, this is a difficult prospect. (Racing Thoroughbreds and Standardbreds are best suited for this type of business.) Before you jump into the breeding business, put pencil to paper and figure out the costs.

There are two ways to breed: Either you breed your mare to a stallion owned by another party, or have your stallion bred to someone else's mares. The latter tends to be the more profitable of the two types of breeding.

BREEDING YOUR MARE

Suppose you own a $3,000 mare, and you want to breed her.
- You breed her to a stallion whose stud fee is $900.
- The costs of caring for the mare while she is being bred total $300 (if she catches the first time you send her).
- It costs roughly $1,000 to maintain the mare for the 11-month gestation period.
- Delivery goes smoothly and you don't have to call in the veterinarian. When the foal hits the ground, you already have $2,200 invested.
- It will be two years before you can begin to train the horse to saddle, at a conservative cost of $2,500.
- Upkeep of the horse while you break it yourself, or send it away for training, costs another $700.

Your total investment = $5,400

This is the estimated amount that must be invested in your two-year-old horse. It could be higher or lower according to your particular situation, but the estimate here is conservative. The total selling price you'll need just to break even is more than the cost of the dam. The colt still must be shown, promoted, and advertised before it can be sold, and that costs money, too.

Breeding this mare and trying to sell her colt for a profit just doesn't make good financial sense. In general, the vast majority of owners will lose money in this situation. If you really want to breed one of your mares, consider the investment and potential profits or losses first. Don't make an emotional decision. Although your favorite mare has served you well, her most profitable future may not be as a brood mare in your barn. If you really want to keep her, you may be able to lease her out to someone else for breeding purposes. If she produces some real stars, take her back, breed her, and sell her offspring as yearlings.

Another option is to help offset the costs of a foal by using it as a teaching tool. This is covered in more detail under the section "Integrated Systems" in Chapter Three. For example, you can hold a hands-on clinic, teaching students how to halter-break a foal, or a six-month course on how to break a colt to saddle.

BREEDING YOUR STALLION

This type of breeding operation requires less capital and fewer (if any) mares. It can generate a positive cash flow in far less time. The primary source of income here is from fees paid by mare owners to have their mares bred to your stallion — the stud fee. Mares are brought to your farm, and their owners pay you for stud fees and mare care fees.

The principle goal of a completely commercial breeding operation is to breed as many mares as your facility and stallion can handle. Generally speaking, the commercial life of a stallion in this type of operation is three to four years in any one region. While a stallion may still be profitable after that time, the demand for his services may begin to decline. The length of time during which a stallion is commercially viable will vary, depending on breed or horse type and the period of popularity.

Many breeders will combine both types of breeding. They will buy a stallion to breed to mares from other barns as well as their own. With most show horse breeds, the most profitable operations breed largely to outside mares. This is especially true for small breeding operations. However, having a few good mares with foals in your barn is a good way to promote your stallion.

♘ If you have the right stallion and promote him properly, it should not take long to recover your investment in him.

Know Your Market

Understanding the market means knowing first and foremost if there is a demand for the type of stallion you want to buy and breed. What is the current population of this breed in the area? (National and state breed organizations, local horse councils, or the Cooperative Extension service can provide you with information.)

Research the competition by attending area breed events such as shows and races. What breeds are popular? What are their stud fees? How many mares were bred in the previous season? Much of this information is available in newsletters or simply from talking to people. Try to learn as much as you can from mare and stallion owners.

After you have completed your research, plan your marketing strategy. Review the information you have to determine if there are gaps in the area's stallion market; these gaps might be for specific types of horses, horses with certain bloodlines, or stud fees for types of horses within a certain range. For instance, there may be several stallions of a certain type in one region, but they are all standing for high stud fees. You may be able to fill a niche in that market by standing a stallion of similar quality for a lower fee.

If there are no gaps, look for areas in the market in need of a good horse. A good example of this situation is in the cutting horse industry. There are now many daughters and granddaughters of the great horse Doc Bar. Many stallions in the cutting horse industry are sons and grandsons of Doc Bar. The owners of the Doc Bar mares are looking for good stallions with different bloodlines to which they can breed these mares. Some breeders who saw this trend developing introduced into the market the right kinds of stallions and are now reaping the benefits of their foresight.

Consider the demand for young horses of the type you want to breed. What would be the market value of your stallion's get (offspring), and at what age will they bring their best price? For answers, read about or attend public auctions. Purebred consignment sales can provide substantial information about the value of different types and ages of horses. If you're interested in a special type of horse (dressage, five-gaited, for example), find out its average sale price. Some auction companies will provide you with sale price averages and ranges for the various horse types they handle.

Stud Fee Determination

The number of mares booked to your stallion will depend largely on the stud fee. The lower your fee, the more mares you'll breed. Assume that you have just bought a stallion, Silver

Lightning, a popular sire in the West, and that you will bring him to the East Coast for the next breeding season. You may be tempted to think, "Silver Lightning bred 50 mares and his stud fee last year was $1,500; there should be no reason why he can't do that in the East."

More often than not, however, that line of reasoning results in a shortage of outside mares coming into your barn. Although Silver Lightning may be an exceptional horse that is widely known throughout the West, most people elsewhere will not know about him at all. If you charge a special introductory fee of $650 to $800, you stand a better chance of breeding him to a large number of outside mares.

The same logic applies to the young stallion that has not had the chance to prove himself as a sire. In fact, you may have to keep the stud fee low until his get have the opportunity to prove themselves. The only exceptions may be stallions that have earned a reputation as outstanding performers in the show ring or on the race track, and owners of stallions who would prefer to breed a smaller number of mares the first year or two.

You may consider increasing the stud fee if you reach or surpass your goal for the number of mares booked to your stallion the first year. This would certainly be the case if, during the first season, you had more mares than your program could easily handle. While your first impulse may be to increase the stud fee considerably, don't do it. Increase the fee gradually.

Let's go back to the example of Silver Lightning. Assuming that you reach your goal for the number of outside mares bred, you may increase the stud fee by $100 to $200 without losing many bookings. You can continue this annual increase until the first year that the stallion does not reach your breeding goal for outside mares.

If you still have people breaking down your door after increasing the stud fee gradually, you can raise the price more rapidly. On the other hand, you should maintain the stud fee at its current level after any year you fail to meet your goal for the number of mares booked to your stallion.

Consider the following when setting stud fees. The emphasis placed on each will vary with the individual situation.

Competition. What stud fees are stallions of similar quality getting in your region? This is a time to put aside your ego and personal preferences and take an objective look at your stallion.

Consider the Mare Population. How many potential customers do you have? Many stallions and few mares could create a "price war," or it could force many stallions out of the market. On the other hand, a large population of mares that are potential crosses for your stallion may enable you to pick and choose.

♘ *You can't expect to take a share of the market if you price your horse out of its league.*

When considering the mare population, try to predict how far people will be willing to haul their horses to breed to your stallion. A larger geographical region will obviously provide you with a larger number of potential customers. Do not assume, however, that your stallion will attract mares from great distances.

Consider Mare Quality. If your stallion is valuable enough to attract quality mares, you may prefer to breed a smaller number of good mares per year. You can reduce the number of mares by advertising a higher stud fee or a stud fee arranged by private treaty. Generally, the mares eliminated from your stallion's book will be mares of lower quality. A reduction in the number of mares bred per year may reduce your annual income, but foals by your stallion will be worth more money if they are coming from better quality mares.

Your Stallion's Get. It is important to look at the show or race records of horses produced by your stallion and to know the selling prices of these horses. If you price the stud fee at $2,500, but the foals are only bringing $1,500, you're going to lose much of your business. If the stud fee is $500 and the foals are selling for an average of $1,500, you'll be in a significantly stronger position as you develop the marketing strategy for your breeding program.

Special Discounts. Few stallion owners charge the full breeding fee for all mares. Most will give certain discounts for mares who are proven performers or producers of foals that have been successful in the show ring or on the racetrack; mare owners who book several mares to your stallion; and local mare owners or members of local clubs or organizations.

A special situation exists for the stallion owner who is looking for a particular type of mare to breed. If you are breeding hunters, jumpers, cutting, dressage, or reining horses, consider giving discounts to the members of the national and regional organizations that promote the particular type of horse you want.

Financing. Some owners may want to breed their mares to your stallion but can't afford to pay stud fees all at once. Many of these potential customers will book their mares to your stallion if you allow them to pay the stud fee in installments. Financing the stud fee has become an increasingly popular practice over the last few years and will be used more frequently in the future.

There are a number of financing plans. You can divide the fee into three payments, with the first one due when the mare is booked, the second due when the mare leaves your farm, and the final payment due when the foal is born. Alternatively, you might use a more conventional financing schedule that includes a down payment and monthly, bimonthly, or quarterly payments over a certain period of time. You must also decide whether to add interest charges.

♘ *If you think offering financing will bring in more mares, try it.*

If you feel that a standard plan will not be sufficient for all of your customers who want to finance the fee, consider arranging financing on an individual basis or offering your customers a choice of two or three plans.

The value of financing the stud fee is partially dependent on the stud fee itself. Many people will use financing to breed their mares to higher-priced stallions they feel will give them better foals. This line of reasoning may even hold true for stallions with stud fees of $500 or less. Offering financing on stud fees will allow for income from your breeding operation to be spread more evenly throughout the year. However, if your breeding operation produces only a marginal profit or no profit at all, financing a majority of the stud fees may prove to be a disadvantage. You may not have sufficient cash flow to pay the extra bills incurred during the breeding season. Under these circumstances, it's a good idea to require payment of the mare-care bill when the horse leaves your farm. If you do offer terms, finance the stud fee only. Be sure to have a financial plan and understand your cash flow position before making these decisions.

Promoting Your Stallion

"An ounce of image is worth a pound of performance." That old saying is as true in the horse business as it is anywhere else. You may own an outstanding stallion, but if you can't project that to your potential customers, your stallion won't have the opportunity to be proven as a sire. Remember, design all promotion to provide the maximum exposure for your stallion at the lowest possible cost.

An effective marketing strategy is the cornerstone of many successful breeding operations. It is not something that is done in a haphazard manner if you want to maximize cost-effectiveness. Instead, organize your approach:

- Analyze your stallion.
- Set long-term and short-term goals for your enterprise.
- Promote your breeding operation.

Analyzing Your Stallion's Assets

Examine your stallion's assets before planning your promotional campaign. This analysis should be based on pedigree, performance, conformation, disposition, and producing ability. An attractive stallion with a strong pedigree and impressive performance and siring records will be the easiest horse to market. However, this situation rarely occurs, which means that some extra work will have to go into your promotional campaign.

U Plan your advertising to reach the most likely prospects.

- Study the pedigree. Get as much information as you can concerning the performance records of your horse's ancestors for at least three generations. If the only well-known horse is a great-grand-parent, still include that in the list of assets for your stallion. While the record of an ancestor three or four generations back is usually of little genetic value, it does have marketing value.

- Look at your horse's lifetime performance record. If he was most successful as a young horse (weanling or yearling), make sure you add that to the list. State and national awards look good in advertising.

- Emphasize the strongest points of your stallion's conformation. List any superior conformation traits he passes to his offspring and his offspring's performance records.

- Don't forget disposition. This characteristic is an especially important one for many mare owners.

- Set long- and short-term goals for your stallion (see Chapter 3).

In addition to implementing the ideas for advertising and promotions outlined in Chapter 2, there are three options to consider for the breeding operation: stallion service auctions, futurities, and promotional syndicates.

Stallion service auctions. Your area breed organization may sponsor a stallion service auction each year as a fund-raiser. Stallion owners each donate a service by their stallions to the highest bidder to raise money for the organization. Each owner must breed a mare for free, but they all get promotional mileage in the process. The donation does not include mare-care costs; the mare's owner is still liable to the stallion owner for these expenses. The stallion owner makes a profit from care of the mare.

These auctions can be set up in different ways. Some groups hold them as regular auctions, where you bring your stallion. This arrangement benefits the unknown or unshown stallion. More mare owners will have a chance to see him at the auction than if he stayed at the farm. If the stallion service auction is operated in this manner, your stallion will get great exposure.

Other methods of conducting a stallion service auction include a mail bid system and an auction connected with a social event.

Auctions are an effective avenue for promoting your stallion. If you can't bring the stallion to the auction, at the very least attend and organize a promotion.

- Mount several pictures of your stallion and his offspring on blackboards.
- Erect a display table stocked with promotional materials.
- Show slides or a video presentation of your stallion.

Most stallion service auctions provide a catalog of their stallions. Have a good picture of your horse published and, through a footnote, acquaint the public with his strengths by listing pedigree, performance, and sire record.

If your local breed association doesn't have a service auction, generate some interest and try to get one started.

Futurities. A futurity is either a race or a show in which the horses are entered before they are born. The sire and/or dam is nominated in advance so that the foal has an opportunity to enter the futurity. Payments are then made periodically by the person who nominated the foal, until the event takes place. Often, the owner of the mare will nominate the foal, pay into the futurity, and show the foal with the hope of winning money.

Many futurities are worth large purses. The All-American Futurity is one of the world's richest horse races, and the winner takes home over $1 million. There are also halter futurities, cutting futurities, reining futurities, and pleasure futurities for many stock horse breeds. There are even futurities for Welsh ponies. The races and shows may operate at the local, state, regional, or national level.

How does a futurity help promote your stallion? The answer is simple: People would rather win money than ribbons. By breeding their mares to your stallion, they have a chance to win money.

Be an enthusiastic supporter and promoter of futurities. As you work to stimulate interest in them, interest in your stallion also will increase, especially if he sires futurity winners. Make sure any advertising or promotional literature about your stallion includes the names of the futurities in which your stallion's get are eligible.

Promotional syndicates. An event that is starting to gain prominence, especially in the Quarter horse industry, is the promotional syndicate. Several owners own one stallion and share costs and profits. Special cash awards are offered to winners of certain events exclusively for the get of the stallions in the syndicate. More information about syndicates can be obtained by talking to breeders and to veterinarians who service breeding operations, and from reading breeding magazines.

Futuries and similar events that pay sizable purses will increase in popularity. Take advantage of this trend.

10
Farm Property and Maintenance

You may already own or lease land for the site of your horse business and have all the space and facilities you need. If not, the first section of this chapter is for you. If you are already an established horse business, the latter part of this chapter will help you maintain your farm as cost-efficiently as possible.

SHOPPING FOR PROPERTY

To thrive, horses need adequate pasture to graze and space to move around. They will need shelter from bad weather. If you plan to stable them, they will need adequate indoor space. Buying land to build a farm or leasing an existing farm is no small investment, so you'll want to make sure you make a good selection. More details are provided later, but keep the following important considerations in mind as you evaluate properties:

- Size and type of horse business you plan to have, including expansion plans
- Types of facilities you'll need, such as indoor and outdoor riding rings, a stadium, or cross-country courses
- Location, including public services, such as garbage and sewer, adequate water, and easy access to trails
- Proximity to neighbors
- Population in the area and whether it's large enough to provide clientele for a horse business
- If you are considering taking over the site of an existing horse business, was it profitable, and if not, why? Did it have a bad reputation? Can you realistically overcome the problems your predecessor had?

Space Requirements

Adequate pasture for horses to graze will keep your feed costs down and make your operation more cost-efficient. In many areas, two acres per horse is ample, but if the soil and grasses are of poor quality, you'll need more acreage per horse. For instance, on some of the rangeland in the Southwest, about five acres per horse is needed, but the land costs less than it does in other areas.

Land Characteristics

It would be preferable to have land with trees in the pastures to shade horses from hot sun and provide a wind break. Make sure, however, that the land does not have trees and other vegetation that are poisonous to horses, such as wild cherry, yew, deadly nightshade, and red maple. Fruit trees, especially apple, could also pose a problem if horses eat too much of the fruit and develop colic.

Sometimes, hilly land may be less expensive because it is not as suitable for development. It also provides good drainage if erosion is not a problem. But if you are considering a hilly site, make sure there is enough flat land for buildings and rings.

Land in a floodplain can be a good value. Floodplains may extend for miles and provide extensive areas for trail riding without the threat of urban encroachment. A friend purchased pastureland in the 100-year flood plain in Virginia (the land had flooded in the last 100 years and thus cannot be built upon). She paid $7,000 an acre. Her sister bought adjoining property that was not in the flood plain, and paid $100,000 an acre.

The bottomland in these areas is usually very rich and can sustain more horses per acre, but there are pitfalls. If the land is wet most of the time, your horses could develop hoof problems such as cracking, thrush, and mud heels, not to mention pulled shoes. Mosquitoes, flies, and internal parasites could present problems. The most obvious drawback is that you'll need to have an escape route if the area ever floods again. If the parcel is covered by the Wetlands Protection Act, an environmental law, you may be prohibited from building on it or clearing parts of it. With all there is to consider, it is imperative that you check with local authorities to see just what laws and regulations would affect the property and a horse business.

Considering that a horse drinks from eight to ten gallons of water daily, it would be advantageous to have a creek running through the property or a pond to help reduce labor and water costs, especially if you are paying by the gallon. However, ponds should be fenced off if you are in an area where winter temperatures reach the freezing point to avoid horses falling through ice.

Soil type can be important, but you may not have much of a choice. Generally, soil with a high percentage of sand will drain better than will soil laden with clay.

Money-Saving Tip
You can make your business even more cost-effective if you have adequate space and conditions for hay production.

♘ *Sandy soils are likely to make for easier going on horseback during wet spells, and they don't become compacted during dry spells, which can be hard on legs and hooves. Sandy soil is certainly better than heavier soil for riding rings.*

Ross Chapple

A run-in shelter offers horses protection from sun, freezing winds, and driving rains.

Barns

The subject of barns could take up an entire book, but there are some important points worth mentioning for anyone contemplating building or refurbishing a barn. It usually is less expensive to buy or lease property with an existing barn. Building costs today are high, especially if you cannot do most of the work yourself. In some areas, the cost of a simple four- to six-stall barn can run more than $20,000.

If you do build a barn, try to make it compatible with the neighborhood architecture. Attractive paint colors and tasteful landscaping can make a less expensive barn look better than it actually is, and it will please your neighbors. Architectural appropriateness will be more of an issue as farms become swallowed up in urban sprawl. My sister, for instance, lives in a lovely Victorian neighborhood that has a stable within the development. Normally, no one would paint a barn Victorian olive green, but it makes this horse business fit in beautifully with the surroundings.

Also, visit large and small barns in your area. Notice what layouts work well, features (such as wash stalls) that are well used, and the size stall that seems to work best. If you are in an area with a cold winter climate, notice which barn designs retain heat. For warmer climates, you'll want to consider barns that stay cool in summer.

- Use low-maintenance, long-lasting materials, such as pre-painted vinyl or aluminum siding instead of wood, to save on repainting costs.

- Compare prices of products and contractors. Prices can vary dramatically from one supplier to another, whether you are shopping for lumber or an electrician.

- Plan for future expansion. A profitable operation will grow and require more space. Leave yourself plenty of growing room.

- Build it yourself or have students build it. The Cooperative Extension Service has blueprints for small buildings available to you at no cost. In addition, many high schools have vocational courses in building trades. You may be able to have the students build the barn for the price of materials only. Often the school's shop teachers get supplies at a discount, so it pays to establish good relationships with local educators.

- Lay out plans to ensure a labor-saving facility. Centrally locate the feed room. Have openings in the stalls that enable the staff to feed and water from the aisles. My sister-in-law had a carpenter cut trap doors in the hayloft so that hay can be fed directly into the stalls. The trap doors are equipped with handles so that it isn't even necessary to bend over to open each door. This eliminates the need for hauling or tossing bales down and carrying them around.

- If you plan to have a lesson or stud barn, design stalls with doors that close in the aisles so that horses cannot reach out and bite when other horses are being led through. Have feed buckets installed so that horses in stalls next to each other will be on opposite sides of their stalls when eating; otherwise, it can cause tension and wall-kicking. Design stalls so that the staff can feed through the stall wall without having to open the door, thereby risking injury walking a bucket of feed to the back.

- If you plan to include a washroom, invest in a brushed concrete floor to prevent slipping. To draw off water, include a drain, and design the floor to be elevated about one foot above the outside ground level.

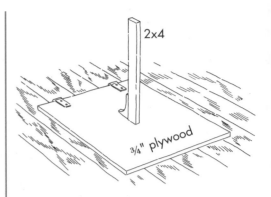

Install trap doors in the hayloft to save on labor: hay can be fed directly into the stalls.

Outbuildings and Other Facilities

The list of other facilities and outbuildings could be a long one. Some of those you may seriously want to consider include a place to store hay if there isn't one in the barn; an office; and rest rooms for clients, with a shower if possible. You may need a place to park tractors, trailers, and vans, as well as a parking area for clients, depending on the type of business you plan to operate. Other especially important considerations are outdoor shelter and fencing.

Outdoor Shelter. Horses that are turned out for long periods or that live permanently outdoors need a run-in shelter. This protects them to some degree from sunburn and rain rot on their skin, and from hoof problems such as thrush, pulled shoes, and dryness and cracking. The main purpose of shelters, however, is to protect horses from freezing winds and driving rains.

Shelters should face south to avoid cold north winds. When I was growing up, my grandfather had a toolshed that faced north, and I converted it into a stable for my Shetland pony. In rainy weather, the pony could have stayed dry standing in the shed, but he preferred to stand in back of the shed to block the wind. In cold weather, I would often go out to knock icicles from his whiskers, lead him into the shed, and give him a warm bran mash, only to watch him promptly leave the shed and stand outside in the elements. My point is that horses would rather be wet than have cold wind blowing on them, so be sure to build shelters facing south.

The run-in shelter should be elevated enough so that the footing stays dry. It should be large enough to accommodate all horses that want to come in without resulting in a fracas. Usually, about 140 square feet per horse is adequate for a run-in shed.

FENCING OPTIONS

Type	Maintenance	Pros/Cons
Electric	low	Costs less than many other types of fencing. Requires power; horses could become impaled on low posts or entangled in wire.
Wooden	high	Attractive, but is high maintenance and can cost a lot. If not maintained, horses can become impaled on broken boards or injured by nails. They can also ingest wood if they chew on boards.
PVC	very low	Requires virtually no maintenance and has few if any hazards. If horses bump into it, it gives. But it's very expensive.
Steel pipe	moderate	Prices vary widely depending on the geographic location. Requires welding at posts. Must be painted periodically with rustproof paint, and if horses collide with it, it won't give.

If you live where the weather is temperate most of the year, trees might provide adequate protection in cool and warm weather. You'll save on the costs of constructing a run-in shed, on bedding for the shed, maintenance of the shed, and injuries that sometimes occur when several horses all try to get into one shelter.

Fencing Options. There are a wide variety of fencing options available. The primary consideration, of course, is safety. Barbed wire is a poor choice, since it can be a source of serious injuries to horses.

I favor wooden fences. They can be expensive and require regular maintenance, but they look very attractive running the length of a pasture. If you select wood fencing, be sure the rails are on the inside so that horses can't kick them out and to lessen the chance that foals will injure their legs on the posts.

Steel pipe fencing with steel posts is another good choice. Make sure the welds are smooth. Cover the entire fence with antirust paint. Instead of using a brush, apply the paint by rubbing it on with a thick rubber glove — it's easier.

Polyvinylchloride (PVC) is popular in some areas. It is generally installed with concrete posts, and is virtually maintenance-free. The PVC rails "give" a little when bumped by horses, which reduces the likelihood of injuries.

Electric fencing can be effective in separating areas within a pasture, but I don't recommend it for widespread use around an entire field and especially wouldn't use it along a road. If horses are frightened and running hard, they'll go through the

If you choose post-and-rail-fencing, be sure the rails are on the inside so that horses can't kick them out.

Premier Fencing Co.

Electric fencing is easy to install and fairly inexpensive. However, it is not recommended for use along busy roads.

fence. If you have any electric fencing on your property, be sure to put up a warning sign for people.

Before investing in fencing, talk to other horse owners to find out which type seems to hold up best in the area's climate and which type is the most economical. Then comparison shop among fence vendors.

Legal Considerations

Before purchasing or leasing a site for an equestrian operation, check with the planning commission to see what the future holds for your area. What are the plans for sewer and water lines? Are there statistics indicating what the growth will be in the region? A rising population could help a riding lesson stable by increasing the number of potential students, but it could hinder a public trail riding stable if access to trails is lost in the course of developing housing. Ask if there are any livestock restrictions that could hinder your business operation. Has anyone else submitted plans to open a riding school nearby? Are there any major roads planned that would increase the value of the land and thus raise your property taxes? This kind of change could bring in more business, or it could cut up your property and decrease its value or make the property worth more but raise your taxes.

In the long run, it may be more profitable to purchase land that costs more initially but is located in a more profitable area rather than buying a cheaper parcel that is so remote that there are not enough people around to support your business. The profit potential of the property's location must be fully investigated and projected before you make a purchase. Even the best book on farm business management will do you little good if you have no clients.

After all these considerations, don't forget to learn about all the permits you'll need for an equestrian operation. Zoning regulations, building permits, environmental laws for waste disposal, wetlands regulations, and, if applicable, homeowners association rules need to be checked. Easements may exist. Where I live, there is a gas easement behind the house and even though my husband and I own the property, there are restrictions about how close we can build and dig near that easement. Often, no one tells you these things; you must ferret them out yourself.

Leasing Property

If you don't have much money to spend on property, you aren't sure you want to be in the horse business forever, or you're not certain you can make a living with horses, leasing may be a better idea than buying. Leasing with an option to buy may be the best choice of all.

⚘ You'll need a title search to be sure you have clear ownership.

⚘ Remember that even if you hire a real estate agent to help find your property, the agent may be paid by the seller. Have a local attorney familiar with all legalities affecting the horse business in your area brief you, check things out, and help you plan your business to abide by all laws and regulations.

Before signing a lease agreement, however, have your attorney review the documents to make sure they are to your advantage. I know of a case where someone leased property and erected aluminum facilities, with the intention of taking them along when the lease expired. This person found out too late about a clause in the lease stating that improvements made on the property would become part of the real estate and could not be removed when the lease was up. Make sure your lease stipulates who has the right to take along improvements.

Leasing with an option to buy can be advantageous because:

- There are no closing costs or agency fees.
- Many banks will not make a loan of more than 50 percent if the property is raw land, or will charge a significant down payment or a higher interest rate. Sellers may be willing to finance the property to you regardless of the amount of raw land.
- Sellers may charge a lower interest rate and require less money down than would a bank. If the sellers are wary of such a transaction, demonstrate on paper how much more they can make with interest on the property, compared with what they would make if they sold through a real estate agent and did not finance the property.

Lease-to-buy options can be disadvantageous when:

- The owner charges a higher interest rate than you can get at a bank.
- The owner allows you to borrow more than a bank would, the amount is more than you can afford, and you end up in default and the seller gets back the property.

FARM MANAGEMENT AND MAINTENANCE

It is essential to provide proper maintenance of your facilities. You'll reduce the number of injuries to horses, which helps keep veterinary bills in check. If your farm is nicely maintained, you also are more likely to keep clients and attract new ones.

Buildings

Routinely check the barn and every stall in it for protruding nails, jagged metal, splintering boards, and anything else that might result in an injury to horses or to people. Check the locks on stalls and gates to make sure they are in good working order to prevent horse escapes.

Make sure the feed room is easily accessible for feeding as well as for deliveries, but install locks that will keep horses out.

For your own protection, hang a disclaimer notice reminding people that you are not responsible for lost or stolen equipment.

Unfortunately, disappearing tack and equipment is a common complaint among boarders. Eliminate headaches by selling tack trunks or making available lockers in the tack room. Door and cabinet locks may deter would-be thieves.

Landscaping

Landscaping around the farm can add significantly to its visual appeal. Be sure to take proper care of trees, fertilizing and pruning as necessary. Cover trees with heavy-gauge chicken wire or fence them off if the horses are chewing on them. (It doesn't take long for a horse to remove a strip of bark all the way around a tree, which will cause the tree to die.)

An attractive flower garden around the stables gives it a professional, welcoming appearance. Potted plants dress up jumps when you have horse shows.

Pasture Maintenance

Establish and maintain good pasture. Remember, a well-kept pasture is an inexpensive feed source.

If you need help developing better pastures, contact your county Cooperative Extension Service, which is affiliated with state-operated agricultural colleges. Your tax dollars pay for these services, so use them. Most Extension agents have a wealth of agricultural knowledge and are ready to answer questions. All Cooperative Extension Services have publications, videos, seminars, and youth programs; they'll also perform forage and soil testing. Here are some basic pasture maintenance practices to follow:

- To contain labor and fuel costs and reduce wear on your tractor, train a horse to pull a drag and let students drive the horse over the pastures. You could have them drag rings and paddocks, too. Dragging the manure piles exposes the feces to the sun, which in turn reduces the number of parasites that ultimately could end up inside your horses.
- Routinely check pastures (and paddocks) and remove any debris, dead branches, equipment, poisonous plants, loose wire, stones, and anything else that could prove hazardous.
- Use herbicides and fertilize as necessary. Your local Extension agent can provide instructions, kits, and mailing boxes that enable you to test your soil and determine the quality of your pasture. This is not expensive; a test costs around $10. Some nurseries and feed companies will test for you if you buy from them, but be sure they don't recommend more fertilizer than you really need.

Timothy

Bermudagrass

To maximize the time horses get nutrition from the pastures, plant cool-season grasses (such as Timothy), and summer grasses (such as Bermudagrass), along with winter annuals (such as wheat or barley).

- Mow pastures periodically to keep down weeds and seed heads.
- Practice pasture rotation to avoid overgrazing. Carefully monitor grass height, and when it starts getting short, move horses to another pasture.
- Grazing other species, such as cattle, sheep, or goats, helps break the parasite cycle. Some parasites are species-specific; even if a sheep ingests them, it won't be a good host for the parasites, which consequently will not reproduce. Different livestock also eat weeds and grasses that horses don't.
- Provide pasture grazing throughout as much of the year as possible. Pasture boarding has very low overhead costs (if you don't have to irrigate or pay high taxes), and can be one of your more profitable services. It's also good for horses. Green grass and sunshine benefit horses mentally and physically, especially horses that are stabled often.
- Plant cool-season permanent species of grass (such as fescue, timothy, or bluegrass), summer perennials (such as Bermudagrass), and winter annuals (such as wheat, oats, or barley) to maximize the time horses get adequate nutrition from the pastures. Alfalfa and clover also are good additions. Check with your local Cooperative Extension Service to determine the best planting schedule for your area and for help in choosing plants. Fescue, for instance, has been associated with spontaneous abortion in brood mares if ingested late in the pregnancy.

Bedding

Bedding is a continual and often expensive necessity for a stable, so shop around for the best price. Feed stores are usually the most expensive bedding suppliers. It is more economical to go directly to the source, such as a neighboring farmer or a sawmill.

There are many types of bedding: straw, course sawdust, peanut hulls, wood shavings, and chips all are good. Some companies are recycling newspaper for bedding. If available locally, it may be practical and inexpensive. Check to see if the prices on different kinds of bedding change with the season, and adjust your orders accordingly.

Fire Safety

Every horse owner fears a barn fire. Practice these safety tips to help prevent a catastrophe:
- Keep electrical systems clean and updated.

$

Other Bedding Money-Savers

- The less time that horses spend in their stalls, the less bedding they soil. This is another reason to keep horses outside as much as possible.
- Don't bed the stalls excessively. There will be less waste and less labor required to clean stalls.
- Make sure your barn help knows how to pick the stalls economically by removing droppings and wet spots, but not unsoiled bedding. Inspect their jobs periodically to make sure they are not wasting good bedding.
- Compost the soiled bedding and manure, then put it up for sale. Strip and lime stalls only when absolutely necessary.

Water Conservation

Water is an increasing concern in certain parts of the country. As prices increase and reservoirs shrink, conservation becomes even more important.

- Water rings when the water is least likely to evaporate— early morning or late afternoon is usually best.

- Repair all leaky faucets, hoses, and waterers immediately.

- Install or replace rubber washers as necessary.

- Limit the time allowed at the wash rack.

- Make sure the spray nozzle on the hose at the washstand works so that water isn't wasted when horses are bathed.

- Hang certified fire extinguishers in readily accessible locations.
- Plan and practice horse evacuation fire drills.
- Prominently display NO SMOKING signs in the barn.
- Remove combustible or hazardous materials from the barn.
- Ask the fire department to inspect your facilities and make recommendations.
- Install a pond. It can be used in case of fire as well as for drinking and irrigation.

Instituting a good fire prevention program will reduce the risk of damage and accidents and may decrease your fire insurance premiums. Be sure to tell your insurance agent about any preventive measures you have taken and ask how you can further reduce your fire insurance premium.

Saving Electricity

A great deal of electricity is wasted through carelessness. Being energy-conscious will reduce the amount of electricity you use *and* cut down on your bills.

Electricity Conservation Tips

- Ask the electric company to send a representative to conduct an energy survey at your facility and make recommendations about how to conserve.
- Place {Please, turn off} signs wherever appropriate. Be vigilant about enforcing the policy.
- Put timers on the lights so they turn off automatically.
- Use low-watt lightbulbs. Fluorescent lights are the most economical.
- Purchase lightbulbs that have a lifetime guarantee. Many charities sell these bulbs to raise money. If they burn out, the charities will replace the bulbs for free. However, be sure to keep your receipt and remember your contact.
- The electric company can install mercury lights. These outdoor lights cover a large area, and turn on at dusk and off at dawn. Mercury lights are also great antitheft devices. However, the electric company might charge a monthly rate, so evaluate the cost-effectiveness of this option carefully.
- If you do not need lights on overnight, consider installing lights that are activated by motion detectors.
- Remember to pass your electric costs on to your customers. If you rent your lighted rings out to the public, charge enough to cover your costs and make a profit.

Conserving Fuel

Fuel prices and taxes on fuel continue to climb, but you can save on consumption with careful planning. Practice good vehicle maintenance. Proper tuning, oil changes, tire inflation, and alignment all reduce oil and gasoline consumption. (See the Vehicle Maintenance Form in Appendix H, page 132.) If you have an electric water heater, put a timer on it so that you heat water only when you need it. You could, for instance, set the timer to turn off the heater overnight. Lower the temperature on the heater to 120°F if it is set any higher than that.

Recycling Manure

Manure requires careful management for several reasons. Inadequate manure disposal results in unpleasant, lingering odors around the farm. It also attracts flies. Make sure your farm has a plan for handling manure; don't just throw it away, and certainly don't pay someone to haul it away for you. The production cost of manure is quite high, and manure has outstanding fertilizing potential. Make the most of it by composting and selling manure.

Controling Flies

The two-winged menace known as the fly is annoying to both man and beast and must be controlled in order to keep a pleasant environment in your barn. Clean facilities and good manure management will result in fewer of these dirty pests. There are a number of systems available to help control fly populations.

Repellents for Stables

Some systems spray a fine mist into the stalls and aisles. With this system, a large barrel containing the insecticide is attached to a timer. Insecticide is released at certain intervals into tubing that sprays through nozzles into the barn. The insecticide is harmless to warm-blooded animals. Although this system is very effective, it can be expensive and may be financially viable only for larger operations. Other systems operate from battery-powered canisters that release a fine mist at timed intervals. These work well and are relatively inexpensive, but they require a periodic battery change.

Flypaper is still the most economical way to kill flies. Despite its unsightly appearance, it does do the job. You can now buy large (1- x 6-foot) sheets. Attach them securely to walls and ceilings to eliminate contact with animals or people.

Manure Recyling

- Sell the manure self-serve. Let customers shovel and remove it by the truckload or barrel full.

- Deliver it to nurseries or private homes.

- Bag it and sell it at the local greenhouse.

- Spread it on your own hayfield or garden. Be careful not to spread it where horses are pastured; this can lead to parasite problems.

♘ Be sure to dilute concentrated fly products as recommended by the manufacturer.

Repellents for Horses

In addition to controlling the overall fly population, the horses themselves must be protected from fly attacks, particularly horses at pasture. A horse's fretting causes stress and weight loss; these, in turn, cost you money.

There are a number of horse fly repellents on the market. The most economical products are usually concentrated and are generally found in feed stores and tack shops. Shop around for the best prices, because fly sprays can be expensive.

Consider feeding supplements with insecticide or providing insecticide blocks, although these options might also be expensive. Ask your veterinarian about the fly-control systems that work best in your area.

Provide your horses, and ask boarders to provide theirs, with fly masks, which keep flies off the eyes of horses. These work well in the pasture. You can make your own version of a face protector by attaching strips of cloth to the horse's halter.

11
Cutting Costs on Horse Care

HEALTH CARE

Veterinary costs can add up quickly, underscoring the truth of the old adage: "An ounce of prevention is worth a pound of 'bute'" — that widely used painkiller phenylbutazone. If you are not well versed in the most common and especially serious ailments affecting horses, such as colic and founder, invest in some good horse-care books, consider taking a course or two on horse health care, and routinely talk to your veterinarian about any special health issues affecting horses in your area. Knowledge about horse health will help you develop management practices that can reduce the likelihood that animals on your farm will become ill.

There are other preventive measures that will help keep down medical costs.

Quarantine all incoming animals. This is integral to good farm management. Horses transported long distances often arrive in a stressed condition, which makes them more susceptible to infectious diseases, posing a risk to other horses at your farm. Horses coming from large auctions or shows may have been exposed to a wide variety of diseases and could be carriers. If you do not quarantine incoming or sick horses, respiratory disease and salmonellosis could spread through your barn rapidly.

The main point to consider when quarantining horses is that you don't want infected and healthy animals sharing the same air. If there is no separate building designated for quarantines, then separate the animals in the same barn. Keep the new or infected horses at one end and other animals at the other, with no horses in between. This is a satisfactory alternative to having a totally separate building. However, the most important thing still is cleanliness. The staff should use separate equipment such as buckets, brushes, and mucking tools for the isolated horses. They should also use boots or boot covers only in the isolated stall and not walk into areas where there are other animals without changing footgear. The stall and all equipment should be thoroughly disinfected with

EXERCISE PARASITE CONTROL

Sometimes, internal parasites cause colic, which can be expensive to remedy or fatal. Internal parasite infestation also causes poor feed digestion and makes feeding less economical. Worming recommendations vary from every six weeks to every six months. Rotate paste wormers since different brands are designed to kill different parasites. Check with your veterinarian to set up a regular, effective schedule for fecal testing and deworming.

soap and water or a solution of bleach and water. Horses that come down with diarrhea or fever should be isolated and treated immediately.

If a horse is infected, wash hands thoroughly after handling the sick animal. Take particular care when working with horses infected with *Salmonella,* since this can be transmitted to humans. Keep horses isolated for two to four weeks to ensure that there is no spread of infection.

Require a current Coggins test and vaccinations for all horses boarded at your barn, including your own mounts. Keep accurate, updated health records on all horses. This protects against vaccinating a horse twice just because you can't remember if it is current, or failing to provide the vaccinations each horse needs. Keep sturdy latches on gates and doors and keep feed rooms locked, since horses that get into the feed bin and gorge themselves could colic or founder.

Assemble a well-stocked first-aid kit you can use at home or that includes supplies that can be taken along when traveling. The kit should include:

bandages	tranquilizers*
thermometer	scissors
gauze	disinfectant spray
phenylbutazone ("bute")*	poultice
	leg brace
ice pack	rubbing alcohol
snakebite kit	colic remedy*
twitch	leg wraps
antibiotic ointment	
antibiotics *	*as advised by your veterinarian*

Many of these products can be purchased at discount stores or drugstores.

Train employees to be on the lookout for moldy, spoiled hay or grain, which can make a healthy horse sick. Also, follow a regular worming program and require that boarders worm their horses routinely as well.

Appraise your string to see if there are any horses that are persistently colicky or accident-prone. They should be culled. They can cause you to lose money, sleep, and your reputation. Boarders get nervous when they hear that horses in the barn are colicky or that a horse had colic and died. You can also reduce horse health insurance claims by getting rid of high-risk horses, not to mention the cost of colic surgery, late nights spent nursing sick horses, or the financial loss if an uninsured horse dies.

Have each horse's mouth and teeth examined annually and treat problems. This pays for itself in the long run, because abscesses, wolf teeth — which are premolars, usually in the upper jaw — and points on molars can cause feed waste and training problems. I once had a "problem" horse that had reared and run away with several riders. Upon checking his mouth, I discovered wolf teeth that interfered with the action of the bit. After the veterinarian removed his wolf teeth, the horse's behavior improved and he went on to become a show winner.

Saving on Veterinary Care and Supplies

It pays to develop a good rapport with your veterinarian. Together, plan a yearly health care schedule. Agree on a course of action for colicky horses or foaling mares so you can consult over the phone and avoid the expense of farm calls whenever possible.

In some instances, it can save money over time to seek veterinary care early. If, for example, you call in a veterinarian right away to treat a horse with colic, the condition may not progress to a far more costly surgical emergency. Besides, the veterinarian will give you important instructions to follow until he gets there to treat the problem.

We can glean many ideas from other species in the livestock business when it comes to reducing veterinary costs. The cattle business has practiced veterinary preventive health care programs for years. The farm manager and the veterinarian design a program to ensure routine preventive health care practices. For example, your veterinarian would design a worming, inoculation, and teeth-floating schedule based on the needs of your operation. Because the veterinarian knows when his visit will be, this aids his schedule and budget planning. It also aids yours because when you do your budget and planning for the fiscal year, you'll know exactly when your health care bills will be due. It assists you in planning your labor and horse-use hours because you'll know which days to set aside for inoculations, worming, and other routine procedures. It eliminates such things as accidentally getting to a big show with an expired Coggins test or forgetting to worm your horses because it was such a busy time of year.

Some veterinarians charge a flat monthly fee for this service, which usually ends up to be less expensive than if you just call and have them out when you need them. As a veterinarian studies your

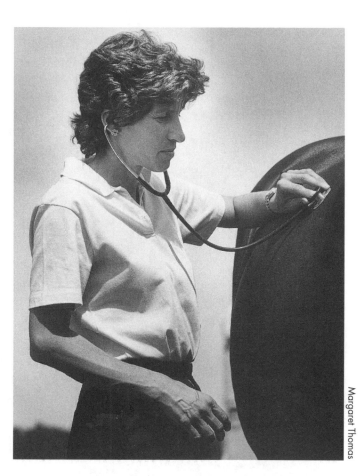

Margaret Thomas

It can save money over time if you seek veterinary care early. Early treatment can prevent an illness from becoming more serious and therefore more costly.

operation, he can also troubleshoot some potential problems that would result in expensive emergency farm calls, saving you even more money.

FEEDING

When a rancher reviews the monthly feed bills, the meaning of "Don't eat like a horse" becomes crystal clear. Feeding horses is no small undertaking, especially considering the dollars involved. If you're in the business to show a profit, it's important to reduce these costs as much as possible.

Consider culling horses that don't earn their keep. Retired or lame horses consume valuable time, resources, and space. Find them good homes elsewhere where they will be useful and appreciated. Gentle horses retired from your school due to age might be a welcome addition to a therapeutic riding program. A horse with too many problems for three-day eventing may be sound enough for the local mounted police unit. Many veterinary schools would welcome the contribution of a horse to conduct research that could ultimately help all horses. Remember that it costs just as much or more to feed an unproductive horse as it does one that is making you money. Following are some other ways to save on feed.

Reduce Feed Waste

Shelter the feed from the weather. Use hayracks to keep hay dry and feed bins to protect grain. Purchase smaller quantities in summer, when insects and humidity increase spoilage.

Screen and lock the feed room. This keeps out eight-, four-, and two-legged pests. In Texas, I've seen fire ants carry off a quarter of a bale of alfalfa in one night.

Routinely worming horses helps prevent internal parasites, which reduce digestive efficiency, rob nutrients, cause colic, and increase the amount of feed necessary to keep a horse at its desired weight.

Regularly have each horse's teeth floated, or filed, to remove points and hooks that form. As horses age, their teeth form sharp points that can cut into their gums. This can result in improper chewing, feed dribbling, and inefficient digestion. Annual veterinary examinations and floating will prevent this problem.

Balance rations. Don't underfeed or overfeed your horses. Keep a keen eye on each horse's condition and adjust the amount of feed as necessary. Mature, idle horses may need only grass or hay. Don't spend money on grain if it's not necessary. Stabled horses performing light work may do well only on high-quality hay, such as alfalfa, or alfalfa combined with grass; horses on good-quality pasture may not need grain, either. Experiment by gradually reducing the grain you are feeding or introduce a less expensive feed source gradually and see if your horses keep their condition.

Have your hay analyzed to determine its nutrient content and how much is necessary to feed each horse. Contact your local Extension agent or an agricultural college for help.

Don't unnecessarily buy supplements and conditioners. A normal horse needs only a balanced ration calculated for his weight and work level. Unless your horse has been diagnosed with a nutritional deficiency or is performing extremely stressful work, supplements and conditioners are unnecessary. Many supplemental products are not backed by research demonstrating they are beneficial. If you're determined to try the latest supplement fad, try the least expensive version first.

Save on Purchasing Feed

- Buy in bulk. Purchase a large feed bin. It will pay for itself in savings, since buying larger quantities of feed is less expensive than buying individually wrapped bags.
- Depending on your barn help, you may want to buy the appropriate weight bales: 100-pound bales are more laborious to lift than 45-pound bales.
- Purchase directly from the feed source whenever possible; it's less expensive than buying from the feed store. But check the quality of any product you buy.
- When possible, buy hay from a farmer when it is in season, and store it in a dry place for the winter months.
- Hay can also be purchased for less if you gather it from the field yourself, thus saving handling costs.
- Buy hay by weight, not by the bale. Not all bales weigh the same.
- Sometimes the same product you buy for horses is sold for less when marketed for cattle. A farmer might try to charge a horse owner more than he would a cattle farmer for the same hay.
- The more commercially prepared the feed product, the more expensive it will be. For example, pelleted feeds cost more than whole oats and corn.
- Corn oil may make the coat shiny, but so does brushing. If you want to feed an oil, go to a fast-food restaurant or supermarket and ask for used peanut oil.
- Make full use of your pasture. Perform a cost analysis to see if it would be more economical to produce your own hay and grains rather than to buy them.

Ross Chapple

Horses with bad habits can be costly investments. Horses that crib, for instance, such as the one pictured above, can damage expensive wooden fencing and stall doors. Horses that weave back and forth when in a stall may be predisposed to leg stress.

SHOEING AND TRIMS

Thousands of dollars are spent annually on shoeing fees. It is well worth the time to review your shoeing needs and the cost to see if there is any way to reduce expenditures. Do not, for example, automatically have every horse trimmed every so many weeks. Hoof growth varies with each horse, much in the same way that people's nails grow at different rates. Have each horse trimmed and shod according to individual needs.

Do not automatically shoe all horses. Some horses and most ponies don't need shoes at all, or only need them on the front feet. There's another advantage to leaving shoes off the hind hooves when possible: Horses are less likely to cause serious damage if they kick another horse during turnout. Use clips, calks, pads, or corrections only when absolutely necessary.

Have the farrier service your boarders on a regular schedule, and ask for a discount for shoeing your school horses.

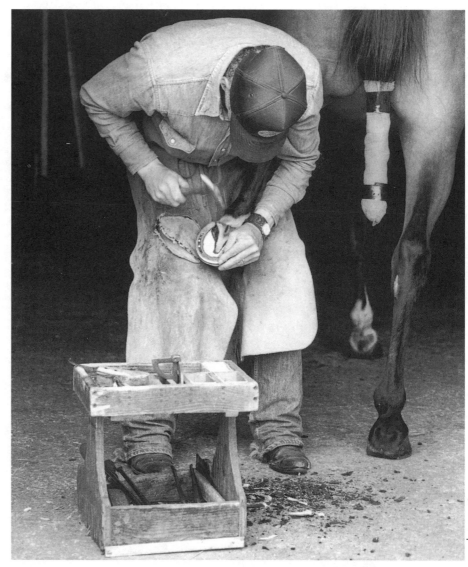

© June Campbell

Try to avoid purchasing or keeping horses with chronic hoof problems. The expense for corrective shoeing, veterinary bills, loss of use, and the time you put in managing these horses quickly adds up.

Finally, if you have a barn full of boarders who are providing your farrier with a good business, ask for a discount for shoeing your school horses. If you have to hold the boarders' horses while the blacksmith puts on shoes, charge for this service. See the Shoeing Chart in Appendix B, page 126, which can keep you organized concerning foot-care needs. It also will enable your boarders to know when their horses were last shod, and it provides a record to use for billing.

PROTECTING YOUR INVESTMENT

Protecting horses on your farm from getting out and becoming lost or from theft is an important part of their care. If the horses are insured, you or a boarder can probably recover economically, but the personal loss often is more painful.

To prevent a horse from getting lost, routinely check the locks on gates and stalls. Check on horses daily to make sure they are all accounted for so that you can take action immediately if one is missing. Quick action will increase the likelihood that the horse can be recovered quickly and safely.

Locating a Missing Horse

If a horse turns up missing, report the loss right away to law enforcement officials. Local owners and neighbors should be contacted in case they saw anything that might help locate the horse. Ask them to help with a search effort. Initiate a telephone campaign to livestock markets and to horse auctioneers in the region. (Your local market can put you in touch with statewide and national market contacts.) These businesses are just as interested as you are in preventing the sale of stolen animals. Direct particular attention at horse auctions scheduled one or two days after the theft. Ask horse traders, particularly those who specialize in handling horses going to the killers, to be on the lookout.

If you have a computer, put out a call for help to contacts over the Internet.

Identification System

A good identification and record system for each horse is invaluable for reporting and locating lost or stolen horses. It also is necessary for insurance purposes.

Age, sex, color patterns, photographs, lip tattoos, pictures or "fingerprints" of chestnuts, electronic chips, muscular dimples, hair swirls, and scars and/or brands may all be used for records and identification.

There are organizations that provide identification record-keeping systems and that also assist in theft cases. Check horse magazines and with your veterinarian for more information. If you have registered horses, contact your breed registry for more information.

EUTHANASIA

Whether to bring an animal's life to an end is an unpleasant decision for anyone, but it's an important topic that must be addressed. Euthanasia may be the kindest option for any animal that is suffering due to serious injury or illness, especially if there is no hope of recovery or for animals that have become seriously and irreversably debilitated due to age. Your veterinarian can help you or your client make the decision and provide information about burial, removal, or other alternatives when a horse is euthanized (or dies of natural causes). You can obtain more information on euthanasia from a brochure developed by the American Veterinary Medical Association; your veterinarian should have copies available.

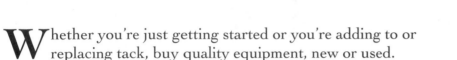

12
Equipment Savings, Opening a Tack Shop

Whether you're just getting started or you're adding to or replacing tack, buy quality equipment, new or used.

SADDLES

Buy saddles that suit your teaching needs. If you are teaching Hunter Seat Equitation, buy flat saddles, not deep forward-seat saddles with huge knee rolls. If you teach roping, you'll need Western roping saddles.

Quality leather will outlast you and your riding school and has excellent resale value; cheap saddles and bridles are more likely to fall apart and can cause accidents.

HALTERS

Leather halters cost more than nylon halters, but they age better, especially if kept clean and oiled, and do not fray or fade. They also break more easily if a horse gets his back foot caught while scratching an ear or gets the halter hung up on something. Nylon halters with leather breakaway straps work well, too. This can prevent serious injury in the stall, the trailer, and the field. I worked with a horse that caught his halter on a large feed manger the night before a show. Somehow he flipped over during the struggle to free himself. In the morning we found him on his back with his head still attached to the feeder. The nylon halter withstood the violent struggles of a 1,100-pound horse. He pulled muscles in his neck and had to have stitches in his face. A leather halter would have broken, enabling the horse to free himself.

Horses generally should not be left in a stall with a halter on, but if they are, be sure the halter is leather or the nylon type with a breakaway strap. The same goes for halters worn in the pasture: use leather or a breakaway.

Tack Cost-Saving Tips

• Discount mail-order catalogs often have great deals on brand-name tack — but buy new only if you can't find it used.

• Ask your tack shop to give you a discount for the business that you send to the store.

• Find and use consignment riding shops. They sell and buy used equipment and clothes and usually have good prices.

• Organize an annual used tack sale/swap. Advertise at other barns in your area.

• Don't throw away old, broken, worthless tack. Even saddles with broken trees, scuffed boots, and cracked helmets can bring in money for display purposes. I sell display sets to department stores, Western wear stores, and Western-theme restaurants. You can do the same.

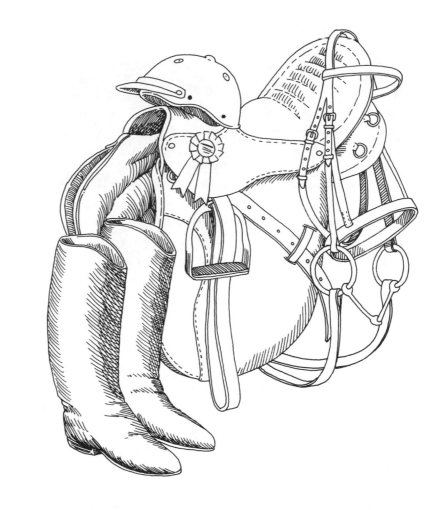

Quality leather tack and equipment will outlast you and your riding school. It will also have excellent resale value.

Try to find inexpensive, preferably used, leather halters. If you opt for the nylon breakaways with a leather head strap and the head strap breaks, replace it with an old leather belt you no longer use or an inexpensive one purchased at a thrift shop.

BLANKETS

Good-quality blankets that hold up are very expensive, so buy these used too, if possible, and keep them clean and in good repair so they'll last longer.

Before investing in blankets consider whether you really need them. Most ponies and horses do not, unless they are clipped for show or are used heavily in the winter. Once you begin blanketing a horse, you'll have to keep doing it all winter long. If you blanket boarder horses, consider charging for the service, because blanketing runs up your labor costs.

JUMPS

The most economical way to obtain good jumps is to make them yourself. There are blueprints available through Cooperative Extension Services. Use a hardwood, such as oak, which lasts longer than other types of wood. Treat the feet of the jump with a wood preservative to prevent rot from constant exposure to the ground.

Jump rails can be quickly and inexpensively made. Purchase 12-foot-long 4x 4-inch posts and have the lumber mill saw off the edges. Mills usually charge only a few dollars each and can do it in little time.

If the thought of building your own jumps gives you chills, ask if you can commission the local high school shop class to build them for you. It will be much less expensive than having them built and shipped from a jump manufacturing company. You might also be able to pick up lumber free if buildings in your area are being torn down.

MAKE YOUR OWN CLOTHES AND EQUIPMENT

New horse equipment and riding clothes are expensive, particularly custom-made items.

Tack shops and horse magazines advertise books on the subject and patterns for making your own riding clothes, horse blankets, and tack. If you are handy with a needle and thread, this can be a real money-saver *and* moneymaker. Monogramming is also popular with horse people. Everything from ratcatcher collars to horse blankets can be personalized. You may also wish to sell cross-stitched or embroidered name labels for chaps or dog collars.

$

Money-Saving Tip

If you sew just for yourself, you'll save; if you sew for others, you can add to your coffers.

TRAILERS

When purchasing a horse trailer, try to buy a used one in good condition. Negotiate the price down as low as possible or do some trading. I once traded a very nice two-horse trailer for an older four-horse van plus a little cash. I had been able to buy the trailer at wholesale cost, so the trade value was actually much higher than the cash invested.

Make sure, too, that the trailer pays for itself. Offer transportation service for horses, ponies, and equipment.

If you are doing a good business with your horses, don't buy too small a trailer or you'll outgrow it quickly. Consider buying a four-horse trailer so you can take three other horses with you to

Offer transportation services for ponies, horses, and equipment.

shows and charge them a transportation fee. This won't cost you more time because you're going anyway, and you can quickly pay off your trailer.

If you spend $3,000 for a used four-horse stock trailer and average one show a month, hauling three horses at $45 per horse, in two years you will have made $3,240. Your trailer will be paid off *and* you will have hauled your own horse to the shows at almost no cost.

COMMUNAL PROPERTY

Another way to save money on equipment is to have communal property. Get a few people to chip in and buy a horse vacuum or clippers. It's even possible to do this with high-ticket items such as tractors, mowers, or a hay baler. See if others in the area are interested. It may be worthwhile to have an attorney draw up some conditions that everyone agrees to, for example, who fixes it if it breaks, where does it stay, how does someone sell her share in the item, and so forth.

OPENING A TACK SHOP

It's easier than you may think. You don't have to open an enormous store if you don't want to, and you already have a built-in clientele, especially if you require riding helmets.

Items for Sale

Consider the capital involved in stocking your tack shop. Expensive saddles might earn you a higher profit, but you may not be able to sell them readily. If you can't sell expensive equipment in about three months, it may be wiser to stock your shop with less expensive items that move quickly.

What to Stock

Experiment somewhat to see which items sell well and which are harder to move. I remember buying a case of pine tar that sat in the tack room forever, as shampoos, fly sprays, and crops went flying off the shelves.

At a riding school, riding clothes do well, particularly for children who outgrow clothes on a yearly basis. Only carry a size line, like 6, 6½, 7, 7½, 8, 8½, 9, 9½, and 10, for boots and one for helmets, sizes 6½, 6⅞, 7, 7¼, 7½. When you sell one, that's when you reorder, instead of having many helmets in inventory. You may realize that you can get by on a more limited size line (6–7, for example), if your main customers are children. Safety vests should be stocked as well in areas where eventing is popular.

Survey your clients and local farms to see what they want stocked, before opening your tack shop.

If many parents wait around for their children to finish lessons, consider stocking magazines about horses and other subjects they could read until their children are finished.

Gift items could be stocked up particularly around Christmas time — books, videos, posters, magazines, monogrammed bracelets and other horse jewelry, model horses, T-shirts, pocketbooks, sweatshirts, and sweaters are all good sellers.

Make a list of items that people ask for, but that you don't have. Begin to stock these, so you won't lose the sale next time.

If someone wants to buy something that you are using just for display, like a jump standard, sell it. It may be an item you want to stock in the future.

Where to Get Stock

The products you want to sell come from two sources: directly from the manufacturer and from a wholesaler. You may need to establish an account with some places, which may be difficult if other tack shops nearby have accounts. Sources may require a large minimum order. But keep trying. The big trade shows, held all over the nation, display every product you could imagine. You can often get discounts for placing orders at the shows, and some "freebies," too. Check in horse magazines or call the manufacturers

- Keep overhead low; try to convert existing space into tack shop space.
- Only stock items that sell quickly, such as crops; a size line of boots; and a size line of helmets. Special-order large items such as saddles.
- Set up a sales display at the horse shows you attend.
- Sell used tack on consignment.
- Sell your barn T-shirts, sweatshirts, belts and mugs. I have found that horse T-shirts sell well year round. They make good nightshirts in winter. (See Chapter 2.)
- Sell paraphernalia from breed associations. Breed associations like those for the Quarter horse and Morgan horse have a variety of decals, posters, caps, and other gear available to promote their particular breed. Contact the breed registries listed in Appendix L, page 146, and see if you can purchase merchandise wholesale.
- Buy horse-training videos. Have them available for rent or sale.
- Sell model toy horses.
- Sell horse books.

of some of the products you have bought in the past and ask the name of the wholesaler.

Stock items that the shop frequently runs out of like fly sprays, ointments, braiding equipment, rain helmet covers, umbrellas, hoof dressings, hoof picks, body brushes, crops, spurs, and gloves. Don't forget veterinary supplies such as bandages, antibacterial creams, wormers, shampoos and mane and tail conditioners, feeds and hay — if you have the storage facilities. Always have your tack shop open at shows, camps, and other events on the farm.

Consignments

In addition to new equipment, a moneymaker in your shop can be selling gently worn tack and clothes on consignment. Some tack shops are *only* consignment shops. This operation keeps your capital investment low. Here's a possible format:

1. Charge a consignment fee. Fees vary from about 20 percent to 50 percent. See what percentage your customers are willing to pay, and adjust your fee accordingly.
2. Set a minimum number of days that you will consign the items, two months, for example; then the price gets lowered by 15 percent. If it hasn't sold in four months, return the item to the owner to avoid tying up valuable floor space.
3. Set a minimum value for the items you will consign, say $30. This eliminates your labor cost on low-dollar items.
4. Have the person come in and pick up the check or give credit; she will be more likely to spend the money made on a consigned item while in your shop, and you'll have a sale in addition to your commission.

Take in used saddles in partial payment for new equipment.

Another moneymaker is a cleaning and repair service for boots, chaps, tack, and blankets. This will bring more business into your shop. If you don't have the time or necessary equipment, contract the work out. Horse blankets can be cleaned quickly at a wand-type car wash. Or you can buy or rent a power washer. Have a blanket wash day and charge everyone enough to cover the rental fee and a profit.

Financial/Money Management for Tack Shop

Use the same principles of budgeting, cash flow, and planning discussed in previous chapters. But here are a few other thoughts.

Separate your tack shop account from the rest of your farm so that you can see if it is actually making money. Then, information for sales and income tax will be readily available.

Keep careful records of what goes to your riding school stock from the tack shop. Bill the riding school and transfer money for payment of goods. When you can't find a crop when you need to school a horse, it's easy just to pop into the tack shop and borrow one. It should be accounted and paid for.

Keep a careful inventory of items and cash flow on your computer. Your accountant will need these receipts anyway and they will be a good defense if the IRS comes to audit.

Pricing Stock

You may be wondering how to price items. Some products have a price suggested by the manufacturer. Books, for instance, usually have the suggested retail price printed on the back cover. Other products normally have a 100 percent markup. You buy for $10 and sell for $20 to cover costs and make a profit.

Tack, though, generally has a lower markup. When you consider how long your inventory may sit on the shelf; your mortgage, electricity, and insurance payments; staff salaries; and set-up costs — even a 100 percent markup doesn't go as far as you might think.

Be competitive. But don't lose money unless it's part of a longer-term plan to lure new customers. Check the prices at nearby tack shops. A loss leader is when a store offers a product at its cost or at a loss in order to bring in new business. You may sell fly spray at cost and advertise your price just to get people into your store in the hopes they will buy something else.

Accurate record keeping is vital. Have a good computer system so you can call up instantly what you paid for an item and when. If someone comes in and offers you cash for an item at less than the price tag, check the computer. If the item has been sitting in the shop a long time tying up space and capital, it may be worth it to sell it for a little less profit so you can make room for some other products that are more in demand.

Make sure you tell your insurance carrier about your expanded business so that your coverage is complete for employees, tack, stock that you may transport to shows, items on commission, computer, and so forth.

Cash is the best policy. Don't extend credit. Horse people, just like many others, tend to overuse their credit. Most customers will come up with cash or a check if they really want the item. Your creditors are not as kind; they expect you to pay up whether or not your customers do. This includes your own riding school. If you take credit cards, remember these companies charge you about 5 percent of the sale price, so adjust your prices accordingly.

Layaway can be an attractive option to offer clients, but keep it short term.

Money-Saving Tip
Speaking of things getting lost, watch out for shoplifters. Be sure to have the tack shop staffed or locked at all times. It's sad, but many things are actually stolen by disgruntled employees, not customers.

Advertising and Promoting Your Tack Shop

Many of the principles in Chapter 2 also apply here. Have a grand opening sale. Perhaps you can offer a special introductory 10 percent off all items ordered before the opening. Many wholesalers offer discounted pricing for items bought in bulk. The purchase of three bridles may reduce the price by 10 percent. If someone orders one and you order two more for the initial stocking of your tack shop, you make a profit and also get your store stock at a reduced rate. There is usually a shipping fee break as well. The more you order and have sent at one time, the more you'll save on shipping and handling charges.

Don't forget the free advertising you get from press releases (see Chapter 2). Send releases announcing the opening of your tack shop.

Have special sales and events, 10 percent off hunt nights, for example. Provide a spread of wine and cheese. On Dressage Day, have a dressage tea and 10 percent off dressage equipment.

Taking It on the Road

If you're going to shows anyway, take a line of items that are especially useful at horse shows. Think of what breaks, runs out, or is easily lost or forgotten — rain covers, umbrellas, gloves, brushes, saddle pads, hairnets, reins, crops, coat show conditioner, hoof polish and applicators, leads, halters, buckets, maybe one bridle. See what sells the best and next time take only those items to the shows. Shows provide an opportunity to try saddles on horses. Take one.

Have a nice display, maybe a canvas canopy or awning off your trailer. It doesn't have to be very large. Make sure the display is staffed at all times.

Take a few gift items for the poor non-horsey parents, like "I'm a Blue Ribbon Horse Show Mom," or "I hate horse shows" T-shirts as well as a rack of riding clothes. Remember, even if you don't make a big profit, you'll be at the show anyway, and you're publicizing your tack shop and farm.

If you don't want to add a tack shop to your enterprise but think you have the business, consider leasing out some space to an existing tack shop for a branch-type operation. You may be able to make money without having to do much more than sign a lease. Someone else will advertise, set up and run the place, and pay you for the space he is leasing, and possibly a percentage of the profits. That shop may even sell you tack at its wholesale cost.

Appendices

The forms in this section are intended to serve as examples. You are welcome to use them; however, be sure to check first with your lawyer or accountant, as appropriate, to make sure they are suitable for your business.

Appendix A   Boarder Information Form

Appendix B   Shoeing Chart

Appendix C   Equine Lease Agreement

Appendix D   Student Record Form

Appendix E   Camp Form — Sample camp application

Appendix F   Horsemanship Certificate

Appendix G   Video Order Form

Appendix H   Vehicle Maintenance Form

Appendix I   Maximizing Consignment Sales

Appendix J   Organization Calendar

Appendix K   Money Management Forms

Appendix L   Breed and Equestrian Organization Addresses

Appendix M   Equestrian Publication Addresses

Appendix A

Boarder Information Form

Owner's name:_____

Address: _____

Phone: (h) _____ (w) _____

Emergency contact: _____phone: (h)_____ (w) _____

Horse: _____ Date of birth: _____

Breed: _____ Color: _____

Markings: _____

Date of arrival: _____ Date of departure: _____

VETERINARIAN

1st choice: _____ phone: _____

2nd choice: _____ phone: _____

Additional services desired: _____

_____

To protect your horse business, it is imperative that all riders who patronize your barn sign a liability release form. However, liability laws vary from state to state. Consult with an attorney in your area who is familiar with equine business issues to provide you with the liability forms you'll need.

HEALTH RECORD

Vaccinations	Date	Deworming	Date

SHOEING RECORD

Farrier	Service	Amount Paid	Date

BOARD/SERVICES PAYMENT RECORD

Date	Charges	Payments

Appendix B

Shoeing Chart

Codes: T = trim, R = reset, N = new, S = special, P = pads, F = front only

Name of Horse	Jan	Feb	Mar	Apr	May	Jun	Jul	Aug	Sep	Oct	Nov	Dec
1.												
2.												
3.												
4.												
5.												
6.												
7.												
8.												
9.												
10.												
11.												
12.												

Appendix C

Equine Lease Agreement

This agreement entered into on the _____ day of _____, _____ , (date) between
_____(the Owner) of _____,
_____(city, state) and _____ (Lessee)
of _____, _____ (city, state).

    WITNESSETH: Owner does hereby lease to Lessee and Lessee does hereby lease from the Owner
the _____ (color) _____ (sex) known as _____ (horse's name).
The lease shall be for a period of _____months, beginning the _____ day of _____, _____. (date)

    In exchange for the exclusive use of the above-named _____ (mare, gelding, or stallion) _____(horses name) during the period of this lease, the Lessee does hereby agree to assume all responsibilities and to pay all normal and necessary expenses for the care of said horse consistent with the practices of good animal husbandry, including but not limited to board, worming, veterinary expenses, shoeing, trimming, and hauling.

    Lessee warrants that he/she has inspected said horse and agrees to accept said horse in present condition. Lessee shall pay and provide for the transportation of the horse from the Lessee to the Owner at the termination of the lease.

    Owner shall have the right at any time, in person or by authorized agent, to go upon the Lessee's premises to inspect the horse and determine if said horse is being properly cared for and in good health. The title and ownership of the leased horse shall be and remain in the name of the Owner. Lessee shall not sell, mortgage, or encumber this leased horse in any manner whatsoever. Lessee shall not assign this lease nor sublease the horse covered hereby.

    If the leased horse should at any time become missing, lost, seriously injured, sick, or dead, the Lessee shall immediately notify Owner by telephone and subsequently by mail.

    Owner shall not hold Lessee liable for any serious injury or death of the horse arising from events not resulting from negligence on the part of the Lessee or the Lessee's agents. Lessee shall hold the Owner harmless for any injury to persons or damages to any property caused by the leased horse.

    No modification of this lease shall be binding unless in writing and executed by the parties hereto.

    The undersigned Owner and Lessee accept the terms and conditions of this lease and acknowledge a copy thereof.

Owner _____ Date _____

Lessee _____ Date _____

Appendix D

Student Record Form

Name: _____ Date of birth: _____

Address: _____

_____

Phone: (w) _____ (h) _____

Parents' names: _____

Contact in case of emergency: _____ Phone: _____

Doctor: _____ Phone: _____

Hospital: _____

Allergies: _____

Level of riding experience: (Please circle)

Beginner   Intermediate   Advanced   Showing

Number of years riding: _____

Date of session desired: _____

Special instructions: _____

_____

Cost: _____   Paid: _____

To protect your horse business, it is imperative that all riders who patronize your barn sign a liability release form. However, liability laws vary from state to state. Consult with an attorney in your area who is familiar with equine business issues to provide you with the liability forms you'll need.

Appendix E

Camp Form — Sample camp application

Name of camper: _____ Date of birth: ___/___/___

Address: _____

City: _____ State:_____ Zip: _____

Father's name: _____ Phone: (h) _____ (w) _____

Mother's name: _____ Phone: (h) _____ (w) _____

Contact in case of emergency: _____ Phone: (h) _____ (w) _____

Medical concerns: _____

Allergies: _____

    All campers must have their own grooming kit, including a curry comb, mane comb, hoof pick, body brush, dandy brush, and lead rope. If camper doesn't own one, it can be purchased for $_____.
Would you like to reserve one? Yes   No
Our strong emphasis on safety requires all students to wear boots and ASTM–approved helmets.
The helmets are $____ and the rubber riding boots are $____.
Would you like to reserve a helmet? Yes   No   Size: _____
Would you like to reserve a pair of boots? Yes   No   Size: _____
Camp dates desired: _____

Appendix F

Horsemanship Certificate

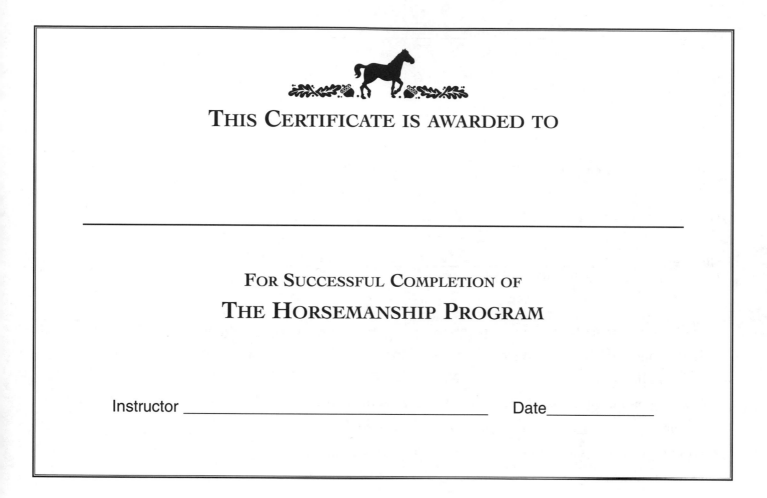

THIS CERTIFICATE IS AWARDED TO

_____

FOR SUCCESSFUL COMPLETION OF

THE HORSEMANSHIP PROGRAM

Instructor _____ Date_____

Appendix G

Video Order Form

Rider's name: _____ Horse's name: _____

Address: _____

_____

Phone: (h) _____ (w) _____

Mailing address, if different from above: _____

_____

Number of copies desired: _____

Horse show, clinic, or lesson: _____

Division(s): _____ Date: _____ Entry #: _____

Classes: _____

Ring #: _____

Special instructions: _____

_____

_____

_____

Signature: _____ Date: _____

Appendix H

Vehicle Maintenance Form

Vehicle _____ Model _____ Year _____

Type of Work	By Whom	Date	Cost
Oil change/lube			
Oil change/lube			
Oil change/lube			
Oil change/lube			
Oil change/lube			
Oil change/lube			
Oil change/lube			
Oil change/lube			
Oil change/lube			
Oil change/lube			
Oil change/lube			
Oil change/lube			
Oil change/lube			
Oil change/lube			
Repairs			
Repairs			
Repairs			
Repairs			
Repairs			
Repairs			
Repairs			
Repairs			
Repairs			
Repairs			
Repairs			
Repairs			
Repairs			
Repairs			

Appendix I

Maximizing Consignment Sales

Dear Consignor,

Enclosed please find a CONSIGNOR'S CHECKLIST for your convenience. This is designed to help you prepare for the Midwestern Quarter Horse Sale. We hope this will help you get the highest possible price for your horse. Many people spend a great deal of time preparing a horse to show for ribbons and points. This auction is probably the most important "show" your horse will attend. It will have hundreds of judges, and the prize will be a check for the value of your horse. So, it's in your best interest to spend time getting your horse well turned out for this sale. If you don't have very much experience selling horses at auction, please take some time to look at the checklist enclosed.

If you have any questions or require any assistance, please feel free to contact Auction Services, Inc. We are eager to help you.

Sincerely,

Auction Services, Inc.

CONSIGNOR'S EQUIPMENT CHECKLIST

✓ Feed and hay
✓ Buckets
✓ Grooming equipment
✓ Halters
✓ A quality halter for showing your horse
✓ A stable halter to leave on your horse for the buyer
✓ Equipment to clean your stall and stable area
✓ Saddle and bridle if your horse is broken
✓ Tools to hang buckets and stall decorations

HEALTH REQUIREMENTS

	Required	Recommended
Original Coggins Report (within 12 months)	☑	☐
Interstate Health Certificate (if out of state)	☑	☐
Soundness Certificate	☐	☑
Broodmares Pregnancy Exam (within 10 days)	☑	☐
Health Records	☐	☑

PAPERWORK

	Required	Recommended
Registration Certificate	☑	☐
Transfer Report (properly signed)	☑	☐
Registration for Unnamed Foals (applied for)	☑	☐
Breeder's Certificate (mares that have been bred)	☑	☐

If a stallion owner withholds the Breeder's Certificate until a foal is born, a letter to this effect, signed by the stallion owner, and a copy of the signed contract must accompany the mare. This will be announced when the horse is sold.

PREPARING YOUR HORSE FOR SALE

❑ Is your horse carrying good weight? (Flesh covers ribs, etc.) *The old horse trader says, "Fat is the best color when you want to sell a horse."*

❑ Is the hair coat in good condition? (clean and shiny)

❑ Is your horse properly clipped? (i.e., muzzle, ears, legs, feet, and bridle path)

❑ Does your horse load and haul well? If your horse has not loaded or trailered, practice before the sale. Plan plenty of travel time in order to avoid rushing and causing injury on the way to the sale.

❑ Are your horse's feet in good condition? (Shod or trimmed. Have this done 1–3 weeks before the sale. Last-minute hoof work may cause lameness without time to correct it.)

❑ Plan to arrive early so that you and your horse are fresh on sale day.

SALESMANSHIP

❑ Bring a saddle and bridle. Show your horse in the performance demonstration. Seeing is believing. (See the attached information on the performance demonstration.)

❑ Stay by your stall to talk to any potential customers.

❑ Keep your stall area neat.

❑ Be pleasant and helpful.

❑ Stall displays and decorations will draw attention to your horse. (Include signs, pictures, trophies, ribbons, scrapbooks, and other information on your farm, including stallion service and other horses you may have for sale.)

❑ Show your horse in a nice clean halter, saddle, and bridle.

STALL LOCATION

❑ Lot numbers will be posted on each stall. Make sure the correct horse is put in each stall. DO NOT MOVE YOUR HORSE.

❑ All of your horses will be stalled together.

❑ If you wish to be stalled with another consignor, contact our office no later than the Monday preceding the sale.

Some Hints on How to Estimate the Value of Your Horse and Handle Pricing on Sale Day

1. When you bring your horse to the sale ring, let one of our handlers take it in. A member of our staff will approach you and discuss your minimum or reserve, if you have one, and relay that information to the auctioneer. He will also keep you abreast of events in the sale ring. If you decide not to sell your horse for the amount bid, tell us before the horse leaves the ring. We will announce NO SALE.

2. DON'T PRICE YOUR HORSE BEFORE THE SALE. It is best to tell potential customers that you want to see what the horse brings in the sale ring. If someone is pushing you to price your horse before the sale, ask him to make an offer. This usually separates the buyers from the lookers.

3. Think carefully about the amount you will accept for your horse. Be realistic and keep an open mind. The best way to determine the value of a horse is to see what it brings in the sale ring.

4. Have a winning attitude. Be positive. You are trying to sell your horse. A potential buyer can sense if you don't like your horse and will figure that he won't either. WE WANT YOU TO GET THE HIGHEST POSSIBLE PRICE FOR YOUR HORSE!

The Performance Demonstration

The performance demonstration is an invaluable tool for selling your horse. If your horse is broken, it will pay to show that in the demonstration.

Helpful Hints:

1. Bring a saddle and bridle that fit the horse.
2. Treat the performance demonstration like a real horse show. Wear proper attire, clean your tack, and make sure your horse is well turned out (mane pulled evenly and braided, if appropriate).
3. Do not use training gear unless it is necessary.
4. Be ready to show early on sale day.
5. *If you do not have anyone to ride your horse, please contact us. We may be able to find a rider for you.*

The demonstration will simulate horse show conditions. Each horse will be introduced individually.

The following classes will be available:

Class 1
Western Pleasure — horses will be shown on the rail at a walk, jog, and lope in both directions.

Class 2
Hunter Under Saddle/Over Fences — horses will be shown on the rail at a walk, trot, and canter in both directions. A course will be set. If your horse jumps, you may move to the center of the area and work over fences after the flat work is completed.

Class 3
Green Broken Horses — shown on the rail at a walk and jog or trot. As your horse is introduced, you may move to the center to jog or lope a circle. Once your horse has been introduced, please move back to the rail.

Class 4
Reining and other horses will work individually. All horses to show will enter the ring and wait to be introduced. When introduced, proceed to the center of the ring as instructed. You will be given a couple of minutes to work. (If there is enough room, two horses will work at once, each taking half the ring.)
WE WILL REPEAT THE CLASSES IN ORDER TO ENSURE THAT EVERY HORSE IS GIVEN AN OPPORTUNITY TO BE SHOWN.

Appendix J

Organization Calendar

Winter	Spring
*Yearly budget and goal planning	*Deworm
*Vehicle maintenance	*Take soil samples
*Organize office; update computer records and filing system	*Fertilize, use herbicide
*Send Christmas newsletter	*Conduct spring break camp
*Have promotional event: tack cleaning or Christmas party	*Advertise summer camps, send applications, hire counselors
*Conduct short course or seminar	*Farm tour; career day
*Do yearly inventory of supplies	*Clinic
*Christmas break camp	*Lease and sell green horses — advertise
*Print applications for camp brochures, prize lists, etc.	*Mail horse show prize lists (see horse show calendar)
*Stationery, business cards, office supplies: update and reorder	*Advertise blanket cleaning and repair
*Train green horses; prepare for spring sale and schooling shows	*Clean and store stable blankets
*Advertise stallion service, Christmas tack, and horse sales	*Organize jump party
*Vet care — vaccinate, blood tests, teeth check, etc.	*Taxes
*Restock first-aid kit	*Facility maintenance: repair, replace, and oil gates; paint, etc.
*Fire-safety drill; check/recharge fire extinguisher, smoke detectors	*Spring schooling show
*Take a vacation!	*Advertise manure sale
*Buy/maintain computer, answering machine, and drink machine	*Plant garden
*Update scrapbook/photo album	*Schedule Photograph Day
*Build cross-country course	*Evaluate school horse string, buy, sell, "tune up"
	*Breed stallions and mares; cull, buy, train

Summer	Fall
*Summer day camps	*Fall lessons
*Horse shows—home and away (send press releases)	*Mock fox hunt (invite press)
	*Deworm
*Clip, drag, and rotate pastures	*Strip stalls, lime, rebed
*Practice fly control	*Check insulation, cover windows, pipes, etc.
*Advertise for mane pulling, clipping, braiding, etc.	*Vehicle maintenance (antifreeze)
*Have square dance, bonfire, ice-cream social, etc.	*Advertise hunter clips
*Vehicle maintenance — coolant	*Send applications for winter session and seminars; advertise
*Evening and weekend lessons	*Reevaluate insurance needs and costs
*Send applications for fall lesson sessions	
*Order hay	
*Order bedding	
*Take a computer class	

Appendix K

Money Management Forms

ANNUAL INCOME STATEMENT

Revenue	Amount	Percent of Total
Boarding rents	$105,000	19.46%
Horse sales	$50,000	9.27%
Commissions	$15,000	2.78%
Camps	$45,000	8.34%
Lessons	$200,000	37.07%
Special clinics	$2,000	3.25%
Horse training	$10,000	1.85%
Horse leases — long term	$20,000	3.71%
Horse rentals — short term	$25,000	4.63%
Breeding/stud fees	$25,000	4.63%
Horse show fees	$15,000	2.78%
Judging fees	$1,000	0.19%
Tack sales	$15,000	2.78%
Book/video sales	$3,000	0.56%
Concessions (drinks)	$1,500	0.28%
Grooming (braiding, clipping)	$3,000	0.56%
Manure sales	$2,000	0.37%
Trailering	$2,000	0.37%
TOTAL REVENUE	**$539,500**	**100.00%**

Operating Expenses	Amount	Percent of Total Revenue
Cost of goods sold		
*Horses	$35,000	6.49%
*Tack	$5,000	0.93%
*Books/videos	$500	0.09%
*Concessions	$500	0.09%
*Horse show (ribbons, etc.)	$4,000	0.74%
Salaries	$100,000	18.54%
Other payroll (SS tax, insurance, etc.)	$20,000	3.71%
Feed		
*Hay	$12,500	2.32%
*Grain	$20,000	3.71%
Veterinarian (fees, medicine)	$3,000	0.56%
Bedding	$3,000	0.56%

CONTINUED ON NEXT PAGE

Operating Expenses, continued	Amount	Percent of Total Revenue
Supplies		
*office	$1,000	0.19%
*barn	$500	0.09%
*other	$500	0.09%
Advertising	$3,000	0.56%
Postage	$600	0.11%
Fuel	$3,500	0.65%
Utilities	$7,000	1.30%
Vehicle repair	$3,000	0.56%
Farrier	$4,000	0.74%
Other	$1,000	0.19%
TOTAL OPERATING COSTS	**$227,600**	**42.19%**
GROSS OPERATING PROFIT	**$311,900**	**57.81%**

Fixed Overhead		
Rent	$0	0.00%
Interest expense	$40,000	7.41%
Insurance	$10,000	1.85%
Depreciation	$40,000	7.41%
Other	$0	0.00%
TOTAL FIXED COSTS	**$90,000**	**16.68%**
PRETAX PROFIT	**$221,900**	**41.13%**
INCOME TAX	**$73,227**	**13.57%**
NET INCOME	**$148,673**	**27.56%**

Cash-Flow Statement

Category	Amount	Increase (+) or Decrease (–) in Cash
Net income	$148,673	+
Depreciation	$40,000	+
Capital expenditures	($20,000)	–
Debt servicing: principal	($16,000)	–
Changes in working capital		
* increase in receivables	$0	–
* decrease in receivables	$0	+
* increase in payables	$0	+
* decrease in payables	$0	–
* increase in inventories	$0	–
* decrease in inventories	$0	+
TOTAL CASH FLOW	**$152,673**	**28.30%**

Income Statement

Revenue	Amount	Percent of Total Revenue
Boarding rents	_____	_____
Horse sales	_____	_____
Commissions	_____	_____
Camps	_____	_____
Lessons	_____	_____
Special clinics	_____	_____
Horse training	_____	_____
Horse leases — long term	_____	_____
Horse rentals — short term	_____	_____
Breeding/stud fees	_____	_____
Horse show fees	_____	_____
Judging fees	_____	_____
Tack sales	_____	_____
Book/video sales	_____	_____
Concessions (drinks)	_____	_____
Grooming (braiding, clipping)	_____	_____
Manure sales	_____	_____
Trailering	_____	_____
TOTAL REVENUE	=======	=======

Operating Expenses	Amount	Percent of Total Revnue
Cost of goods sold		
* Horses	_____	_____
* Tack	_____	_____
* Books/videos	_____	_____
* Concessions	_____	_____
* Horse show (ribbons, etc.)	_____	_____
Salaries	_____	_____
Other payroll (SS tax, insurance, etc.)	_____	_____
Feed		
* Hay	_____	_____
* Grain	_____	_____
Veterinarian (fees, medicine)	_____	_____
Bedding	_____	_____
Supplies		
* office	_____	_____
* barn	_____	_____
* other	_____	_____
Advertising	_____	_____
Postage	_____	_____
Fuel	_____	_____
Utilities	_____	_____
Vehicle repair	_____	_____
Farrier	_____	_____
Other	_____	_____
TOTAL OPERATING COSTS	=======	=======
GROSS OPERATING PROFIT	=======	=======

Fixed Overhead

	Amount	Percent
Rent	_____	_____
Interest expense	_____	_____
Insurance	_____	_____
Depreciation	_____	_____
Other	_____	_____
Total fixed costs	_____	_____
Pre-tax profit	_____	_____
Income tax	_____	_____
NET INCOME	=======	=======

Cash-Flow Statement

Category	Amount	Increase (+) or Decrease (–) Cash
Net income	_____	+
Depreciation	_____	+
Capital expenditures	_____	–
Debt servicing: principal	_____	–
Changes in working capital		
* increase in receivables	_____	–
* decrease in receivables	_____	+
* increase in payables	_____	+
* decrease in payables	_____	–
* increase in inventories	_____	–
* decrease in inventories	_____	+
TOTAL CASH FLOW	=======	=======

PARTIAL BUDGET

Change being considered: _____

(1) ADDED RECEIPTS

    _____ $_____

    _____ $_____

    _____ $_____

    $_____

(2) REDUCED COSTS

    _____ $_____

    _____ $_____

    _____ $_____

    $_____

    (A) ADDED RECEIPTS + REDUCED COSTS $_____ ========

(3) REDUCED RECEIPTS

    _____ $_____

    _____ $_____

    _____ $_____

    $_____

(4) ADDED COSTS

    _____ $_____

    _____ $_____

    _____ $_____

    $_____

    (B) REDUCED RECEIPTS + ADDED COSTS $_____

    (C) NET DIFFERENCE DUE TO CHANGE

        (LINE A – LINE B) $_____ ========

Appendix L

Breed and Equestrian Organization Addresses

American Connemara Pony Society
2360 Hunting Ridge Road
Winchester, VA 22603
(540) 662-5953

American Grandprix Association
3104 Cherry Palm Drive, Suite 220
Tampa, FL 33619
(813) 623-5801

American Holsteiner Horse Association, Inc.
222 E. Main Street, #1
Georgetown, KY 40324-1712
(502) 863-4239

American Horse Council
1700 K Street N.W., Suite 300
Washington, DC 20006-3805
(202) 296-4031

American Horse Protection Association, Inc.
1000 — 29th Street N.W.
Suite T — 100
Washington, D.C. 20007
(202) 965-0500

American Horse Show Association
The National Equestrian Federation of
the United States
220 E. 42nd Street
New York, NY 10017-5876
(212) 972-AHSA; Fax (212) 983-7286

American Morgan Horse Association
P.O. Box 960, 3 Bostwick Road
Shelburne, VT 05482
(802) 985-4944; Fax (802) 985-8897

American Paint Horse Association
P.O. Box 961023
Fort Worth, TX 76161-0023
(817) 439-3400; Fax (817) 439-3484

American Quarter Horse Association
P.O. Box 200
Amarillo, TX 79168
(806) 376-4811

American Saddlebred Horse Association
Kentucky Horse Park
4093 Iron Works Pike
Lexington, KY 40511
(606) 259-2742

American Shetland Pony Club
6748 North Frostwood Parkway
Peoria, IL 61615
(309) 691-9661

American Trakehner Association
1520 West Church Street
Newark, OH 43055
(614) 344-1111; Fax (614) 344-3225

Appaloosa Horse Club, Inc.
5070 Highway 8 West
Moscow, ID 83843
(208) 882-5578

Arabian Horse Registry of America
12000 Zuni Street
Westminster, CO 80234-2300
(303) 450-4748

Belgian Draft Horse Corporation of America
P.O. Box 335
Wabash, IN 46992-0335
(219) 563-3205

Cheff Center for the Handicapped
8450 North 43rd Street
Augusta, MI 49012
(616) 731-4471

Cleveland Bay Horse Society of North America
P.O. Box 221
South Windham, CT 06266
(860) 423-9457

Draft Horse and Mule Association of America
Route 1, Box 98
Lovington, IL 61937
(217) 864-5450

Equine Rescue League
P.O. Box 4366
Leesburg, VA 22075
(703) 771-1240

Lipizzan Association of North America
P.O. Box 1133
Anderson, IN 46015-1133
(317) 644-3904

National 4-H Council
National 4-H Supply Service
7100 Connecticut Avenue
Chevy Chase, MD 20815-4999
(301) 961-2830

North American Riding for the Handicapped
Association
P.O. Box 33150
Denver, CO 80233
(303) 452-1212

Pony of the Americas Club, Inc.
5240 Elmwood Avenue
Indianapolis, IN 46203-5990
(317) 788-0107

Palomino Horse Breeders of America, Inc.
15253 E. Skelly Drive
Tulsa, OK 74116-2637
(918) 438-1234; Fax (918) 438-1232

Railsitter Club
13872 Laura Ratcliffe Court
Centreville, VA 20121-3513
Attn.: Olive Cooney
(703) 818-1644

Tennessee Walking Horse
Breeders and Exhibitors Association
P.O. Box 286
Lewisburg, TN 37091-0286
(615) 359-1574

The American Hanoverian Society, Inc.
4059 Iron Works Pike, Building C
Lexington, KY 40511
(606) 255-4141

The Jockey Club (Thoroughbred)
821 Corporate Drive
Lexington, KY 40503-2794
(606) 224-2700

Welsh Pony and Cob Society of America
P.O. Box 2977
Winchester, VA 22604-2977
(540) 667-6195

Appendix M

Equestrian Publication Addresses

American Farriers Journal
P.O. Box 624
Brookfield, WI 53008-0624
(414) 782-4480

American Saddlebred Magazine and Saddlebred
Horse Association
Kentucky Horse Park
4093 Iron Works Pike
Lexington, KY 40511-8434
(606) 259-2742

Appaloosa Journal
P.O. Box 8403
Moscow, ID 83843-0903
(208) 882-5578

Arabian Horse Times
1050 8th Street, N.E.
Waseca, MN 56093
(507) 835-3204; Fax (507) 835-5138

Arabian Horse World
824 San Antonia Avenue
Palo Alto, CA 94303
(415) 856-0500

Equus
Fleet Street Corporation
656 Quince Orchard Road
Gaithersburg, MD 20878-1472
(301) 977-3900

Horse and Horseman
Gallant Charger Publications, Inc.
34249 Camino Capistrano, P.O. Box HH
Capistrano Beach, CA 92624
(714) 493-2101

Horse and Rider
12265 West Bayaud, Suite 300
Lakewood, CO 80228
(303) 914-3000

Horse Illustrated
Fancy Publications, Inc.
3 Burroughs Road
Irvine, CA 92618
(714) 855-8822; Fax (714) 855-3045

Horse Play
15200 Shady Grove Road, Suite 305
Rockville, MD 20850
(301) 840-1866

Horsemen's Yankee Peddler Newspaper
785 Southbridge Street
Auburn, MA 01501
(508) 832-9638

Horses All
4000 19th Street N.E.
Calgary T2E 6P8
Canada
(403) 250-6633

J.A. Allen & Co. Ltd.
1 Lower Grosvenor Place
London SW1W OEL
England
171 834 0090; Telefax 071 976 5836

Power and Speed
National Grand Prix League
2508 Keller Parkway
St. Paul, MN 55109
(612) 484-9727

Practical Horseman
P.O. Box 589
Unionville, PA 19375
(610) 380-8977

Riding Instructor
The American Riding Instructors Association
P.O. Box 282
Alton Bay, NH 03810
(603) 875-4000

Side-Saddle News
The International Side-Saddle Organization
P.O. Box 73
Damascus, MD 20872
(301) 829-2116

The Chronicle of the Horse
P.O. Box 46
Middleburg, VA 20118
(540) 687-6341

The Cutting Horse Chatter
National Cutting Horse Association
4704 Highway 377 South
Fort Worth, TX 76116-8805
(817) 244-6188

The Florida Horse
5100 W. Highway 40
P.O. Box 2106
Ocala, FL 34478-2106
(352) 732-8858

The International Horse Saddlery and Apparel Journal
Equine Excellence Management Group
P.O. Box 3039
Berea, KY 40403-3039
(606) 986-4644

The Reindeer
National Reining Horse Association
448 Main Street, Suite 204
Coshocton, OH 43812-1200
(614) 623-0055

The Western Horse
P.O. Box 11208
Prescott, AZ 86301
(619) 788-1427

The Western Horseman
P.O. Box 7980
Colorado Springs, CO 80933-7980
(719) 633-5524

USCTA News
United States Combined Training Association
525 Old Waterford Road N.W.
Leesburg, VA 20176
(703) 779-0440

USDF Bulletin
United States Dressage Federation, Inc.
P.O. Box 6669
Lincoln, NE 68506
(402) 434-8550

Index

Telephones
  books, advertising, 14
  use of, 7–8
Television, radio advertising, 15
Theft of horse, 113–14
Therapeutic riding programs,
    47–48
Time management, 19
To do list, 19
Traffic and safety, 48
Trailers, savings, 117–18
Trail rides, 71–72, 75–76
Training
  for counselors, 57
  and sales calendar, 21
  school horses, 44–45
Typesetting, 11

U
Urban horsekeeping, 17
User base, building, 16–17

V
Vaccinations, 108
Variable costs, 31–32
Vehicles
  calendar, 21–22
  and fuel, 105
  and signs, 7
  Vehicle Maintenance Form,
    132
Veterinarian, 108, 109–10, 114
Videos
  for contests, 74
  at horse shows, 47, 68
  for promotions, 16
  for training, 46
  Video Order Form, 131

W
Ware (fox hunt), 73
Washington International Horse
    Show, 68

Water
  and boarding, 50
  conservation, 104
  and property, 95
Western saddle, parts, 61
Wetlands Protection Act, 95
Whippers-In (fox hunt), 73
White pages advertising, 14
Wholesaler or manufacturer,
    119–20
Wooden fencing, 99
Work-study programs, 20
Worming, 108, 109, 110

Y
Yellow pages advertising, 14
Youth riding programs, 17

Z
Zoning board, 5

Other Storey Titles You Will Enjoy

Horse Health Care: A Step-by-Step Photographic Guide, by Cherry Hill. Helps horse lovers master dozens of basic to advanced horsekeeping skills. Explains bandaging, giving shots, examining teeth, deworming, and preventive care. 160 pages. Paperback. ISBN 0-88266-955-9.

Horse Handling and Grooming: A Step-by-Step Photographic Guide, by Cherry Hill. A user-friendly guide for beginners and experienced riders to essential skills including feeding, haltering, tying, grooming, clipping, bathing, and blanketing. 160 pages. ISBN 0-88266-956-7.

Your Horse: A Step-by-Step Guide to Horse Ownership, by Judy Chapple. Packed with practical information on buying, housing, feeding, training, riding, and handling medical problems. 144 pages. Paperback. ISBN 0-88266-353-4.

101 Arena Exercises: A Ringside Guide for Horse and Rider, by Cherry Hill. A one-of-a-kind ringside exercise book for riders who want to improve their own and their horse's skills. 224 pages. Paperback. ISBN 0-88266-316-X.

Becoming an Effective Rider: Developing Your Mind and Body for Balance and Unity, by Cherry Hill. Riders learn to evaluate their skills, plan a work session, get maximum use out of lesson time, set and achieve goals, and protect themselves from injury. 192 pages. Paperback. ISBN 0-88266-688-6.

From the Center of the Ring: An Inside View of Horse Competitions, by Cherry Hill. Covers all aspects of equestrian competition, both English and Western. 192 pages. Paperback. ISBN 0-88266-494-8.

Horsekeeping on a Small Acreage: Facilities Design and Management, by Cherry Hill. Details the essentials for designing safe and functional facilities. 192 pages. Paperback. ISBN 0-88266-596-0.

Your Pony, Your Horse: A Kid's Guide to Care and Enjoyment, by Cherry Hill. This open and inviting guide focuses on all aspects of horse husbandry as well as equine community activities for kids. 160 pages. Paperback. ISBN 0-88266-908-7.

Stablekeeping: A Visual Guide to Safe and Healthy Horsekeeping, by Cherry Hill, photography by Richard Klimesh. Hill shares decades of horsekeeping experience to help readers provide a safe, efficient, healthy living environment for their horses. More than 250 photographs. 160 pages. Paperback. ISBN 1-58017-175-3.

Safe Horse, Safe Rider: A Young Rider's Guide to Responsible Horsekeeping, by Jessie Haas. Encouraging ideas for a good working relationship. Chapters on horse body language, safe pastures, stables, catching, grooming safety, riding out, and more. 160 pages. Paperback. ISBN 0-88266-700-9.

Horse Sense: A Complete Guide to Horse Selection & Care, by John J. Mettler, Jr., DVM. The basics on selecting, housing, fencing, and feeding a horse including information on immunizations, dental care, and breeding. 160 pages. Paperback. ISBN 0-88266-545-6.

The Basics of Western Riding, by Charlene Strickland. An introduction to Western riding. Using clear photographs and illustrations by Elayne Sears, Strickland teaches safe horse handling procedures and basic riding techniques. Trail riding instructions and a complete guide to Western tack are also included. 144 pages. Paperback. ISBN 1-58017-031-5.

These and other Storey books are available at your bookstore, farm store, garden center, or directly from Storey Books, 210 MASS MoCA Way, North Adams, MA 01247, or by calling 1–800–441–5700. Or visit our Web site at www.storey.com.